Praise for Still Standing

As an avid reader and writer, I love hearing stories. What Debbie shares in this book is different. While her story of MS is captivating, it's her matter-of-fact tone and comforting honesty that made me inhale this book. She tells story after story of God's love and grace throughout her life. Read this now. It will leave you with compassion, fortified faith, and soaring hope. It's a celebration of our true Savior who walks beside us every step of our lives.

Christina Hergenrader, Author of *Family Trees & Olive Branches* and eleven more Christian books

This book is going to minister to so many people! I am encouraged by what I've read! The perspective Debbie brings from seeing her story through God's eyes, with spiritual eyes versus earthly eyes, is encouraging and enlightening. *Still Standing* sees life through a different lens, looking forward to being in the presence of God when in heaven.

Rick Ricart, President/Owner Imagine Tours & Travel

I read this timely book about how life events just happen whether you like it or not. It's a must read for everybody who lives in the real world, and nearly all of us do. It's so inspirational to see how faith in God can turn frustration and failure into helping us see the beauty of life and the joy for living.

Carl Landwehr, Founder/Strategic Advisor
Vitae Foundation

Since reading Debbie's story about her struggle with MS, I find myself thinking of her often. She has faced chronic disease with grit and determination, and not just a little awe-inspiring faith. In fact, her perspective is a gift of encouragement for all humanity. Debbie's unwavering trust in a Savior who will never leave her side or let her down allows her to see beyond what is visible to find hope and promise in the wait. Her ability to worship from a four-foot perspective, to find peace from her wheelchair, and to recognize her disability as an agent of the Lord's provision and love, will challenge your thinking and awaken your heart. There is tremendous power found in knowing the ultimate truth. That is, we can count on a Savior who will provide in all circumstances, and who assures us the best is yet to come.

> J. M. Huxley, Award-Winning Author, Podcast Host,
> Speaker, and Nationally Syndicated News Anchor

Still Standing is a raw and real peek into the heart and mind of someone struggling through MS. Debbie's transparent sharing of the fears, the suffering, and most of all the candid questions and wrestling with God is touching. In a strange way, Debbie's story brings hope and encouragement for my faith. I hope you will be encouraged and gain a richer understanding of God's love.

> Rick Boxx, Speaker, Trainer, Author, Founder & CEO
> Unconventional Business Network

Still Standing

HOPE BEYOND DISABILITY

DEBBIE OELKE

Still Standing

HOPE BEYOND DISABILITY

Contents

INTRODUCTION

A Changed Perspective

Cold. Hard. The porcelain tile doesn't give an inch. Lying once more on the bathroom floor forces me to reconsider my resolve to be independent and self-sufficient. All the positive thinking in the world won't lift me to a standing position.

I focus on the situation and determine the specifics of my predicament. Where is the nearest grab bar? Which piece of nearby furniture is sturdiest and able to handle my weight without shifting? Why have I not yet removed that slippery rug whose corner keeps flipping up? What about that unsteady cabinet? It may be perfectly aged and distressed, but does that even matter if its perfectly aesthetic location hampers my maneuverability?

Determination kicks in. Looking around, I consider how to proceed. At least no one can see me. It's not graceful to get off the floor. Should I go to the extra effort of getting on my feet by myself, or should I ask for help? This is especially difficult for me—my legs are weak and almost completely numb because of multiple sclerosis. I barely have the strength to stand. My husband Phil is just on the other side of the wall. Do I wake him or let him sleep? Though I remind myself it is not a sign of mental weakness to call for help, I instead determine to get myself up.

Focusing on feelings of resolve, I gather my mental strength. I must get up. If I stay on the floor, I will have too much time to pity myself. Self-pity is a familiar companion: Life is too hard. I don't like being disabled. I don't like being weak. I do not want to be a burden.

But I will not allow those thoughts now. They will come later, unwanted, as I attempt to quiet my mind when nighttime arrives.

A melody plays in my head repeatedly as I ask the Lord for his help. Though the lyrics of the song, a long-time favorite, mention needing the Lord every hour, I know without a doubt I need him every minute. Every second.

> *I need him every minute. Every second.*

As I start to hum, I focus energy on reaching the safety bar. But my legs are heavy and jerking around involuntarily this morning. As they slide awkwardly on the tile, pain shoots up from the thin covering of skin over my ankle bones. I rely upon my arms, which are not so weakened, to do most of the work needed to get me up. Thankfully, the droning of the bathroom fan drowns out some of my grunts and long exhales.

Once safely upright, more questions come tumbling. Is the Lord seriously good? Even despite ongoing and seemingly unrelenting loss? Why have I experienced troubles of great magnitude without relief? Why have I not been healed?

CHAPTER 1

My MS Story—Well, Partially

"What God says is best, is best, though all
the men in the world are against it."

–John Bunyan, *The Pilgrim's Progress*

Is not the Lord supposed to be the same yesterday, today, and forever? With all the wonderful stories of the feats of God recorded in the Old and New Testaments, and because he is the same Lord and does not change, I must admit it is frustrating that one of these miracles of healing is not apparent in my own life.

To the visible eye, at least.

Will I be disabled the rest of my life on earth? Will I never see healing? Is the Lord asking me to travel this path blindly, without knowing the end result until I reach heaven? Should I put my full faith in him and his mysterious ways? Can I place absolute trust in the maker of the universe?

⚘

I am disabled and handicapped. I can't walk, and I'm not able to move around well. These are hard things to say, but they are true.

> *Can I place absolute trust in the maker of the universe?*

I am a person with a disability because I have had physical limitations the last four years, which have resulted in using a wheelchair just the last nine months. I am considered to have a handicap since this physical limitation presents a disadvantage. The primary disadvantages are my mobility and accessibility; they are almost always difficult.

I lived a perfectly normal life until my disease began causing my physical abilities to decline when I was forty-three years old. And though the request has been laid at Jesus' feet on countless occasions, I am not currently physically healed.

When speakers or singers say that healing is occurring, it obviously has never meant me, at least not to the visible eye anyway. I always wonder if healing is going on—either within me or somewhere else in the room—as the words are being spoken. Truthfully, I sometimes doubt anything is happening during those times.

I know the Lord has the power to heal me, so why hasn't he? Is he waiting for me to go to the right person, the right healer, or the right conference? Is he waiting for me to be around certain people so they can witness a healing? Is he waiting for something in me to be changed? Is he waiting for something in my husband or my kids to be different in order for them to learn some sort of lesson? What is he waiting for? Is he waiting for me to take the right medication? To take the right combination of vitamins, minerals, and other natural products through my naturopath? For me to pray the right prayer or say the right words? Or is this just my lot in life?

Is it a sin to even use those words or wonder about those things?

> " *I know the Lord has the power to heal me,*
> *so why hasn't he?*

The Lord says in Psalm 50 that every animal of the forest is his as well as the cattle on one thousand hills. In other words, he has absolutely no need for anything and he most certainly can do anything. But I have not experienced a miracle of physical healing. Joni Eareckson Tada has rightly noted that the ability to sit in a wheelchair with a measure of godly coping skills is the real miracle. Tada herself became a quadriplegic in 1967 at seventeen after taking a dive that dramatically changed her life. She now is an evangelical Christian author, radio host, and founder of Joni and Friends, an organization promoting the Lord in a community of people with disabilities. She has experience sitting in a wheelchair all day. She has developed patience while learning to interact with others without the use of her arms or legs.

When I asked the Lord for patience, I did not mean I wanted to date a guy (now my husband) for more than five years before getting married at the age of twenty-seven. The lingering span of feeling left behind was excruciating as all my friends and siblings were getting married during those years.

When I asked the Lord for patience, I did not mean I wanted to go through infertility issues for more than four years. I thought the pain of waiting to get married was hard, but waiting to have children was excruciating. Being asked to throw baby showers for expectant coworkers was unavoidable. Being asked when my husband and I were "going to start a family" was not escapable, but perhaps it was preparation for handling uncomfortable questions when becoming disabled. Finally becoming a mother at thirty-five was indeed amazing, but staying at home to parent was also the most difficult thing I had ever done up to that point.

When I asked the Lord for patience, I did not mean I wanted to wait in the realm of international adoption for more than six years, finally getting a China baby when my boys were four years old and nineteen months old. But that is exactly how the Lord did things. That waiting still happened.

And now I am waiting again. This time the desired outcome is healing. I've been waiting to be healed from this major multiple sclerosis exacerbation for over four years now. From the MS itself for twenty-two years.

But it's not about what I want, is it. It is not about my comfort. Life is about what the Lord chooses and about what will be best for his rule. Our Lord is the only God, and he deserves all the glory and praise. He is indeed the one who split the waters.[1] He is indeed the one who brought back Jesus alive from the dead.[2] He performed these mighty acts because it was the right time for *his* purposes. I know he will take care of this major issue in my life when it is the right time and it fits into his design.

This is a story of waiting. But it's also a story of undying hope. Please hear that.

It was the spring of 1997. I was twenty-three years old and about to graduate from the inaugural School of Social Work Master's Program of Washburn University in Topeka, Kansas. During the spring just months before graduation, I started experiencing numbness in my lower body. This numbness was almost symmetrical—it included tingling that started in my toes and moved up my lower extremities. A campus doctor visit resulted in even more questions about what was going on in my body, and I was referred to a neurologist. This specialty of medicine is concerned with the study and treatment of disorders of the nervous system. The nervous system coordinates the central nervous system, which is the brain and spinal cord, and the peripheral nervous system, which includes all other neural elements, such as eyes, ears, skin, and other sensory receptors.

The words "multiple sclerosis" were mentioned by this professional, though I assumed it wouldn't apply to me. Because MS is a very difficult disease to diagnose, and because my symptoms went away after a few months, I was not diagnosed until 1999. That spring, I again experienced numbness. The unwelcome determination resulted from a second MRI, which showed lesions on my spinal cord and brain, as well as from a specialized visual exam and lumbar puncture.

The diagnosis was not a surprise. I have a genetic predisposition for multiple sclerosis because people in my family have had the disease. My paternal grandmother, Luella, and her brother, Roger, had MS. Luella lived until she was only thirty-nine, officially dying of a heart attack since MS itself is not fatal. Her son, my father, was thirteen at the time; she was in a wheelchair for most of his memory.

I wish I could have known Luella and heard more of her story, especially now because I am in a comparable position. Often in my growing-up years and even my adult years, I have been told I physically resemble her in many ways. Having recently realized portions of her story are very similar to mine, I would like to hear her wisdom about becoming disabled, especially coping with the disease while being married to one in ministry and having three children at home.

My father's sister, Karen, said Luella was her hero: "She was full of faith, love, compassion, empathy, and a listening heart and ear. She was non-judgmental and sought out those who weren't as well-received by others." Aunt Karen described her mother as "having a Jesus heart" and went on to say that Luella wasn't defined by her wheelchair; Jesus defined her. My aunt was close to her mother, who was her defender when needed. Luella helped Aunt Karen feel strong and deeply loved. I hope and pray I have more in common with Luella than multiple sclerosis.

I have a small black-and-white picture of Luella as a young adult sitting in a swimsuit with her two sisters. This framed picture has sat next to my bed for years. Though I never met this grandmother, she has always seemed special because of her tragically short life.

I do not know exactly when she started using a wheelchair. The only memory my dad has of her not being in one is when he was around three years old. He can remember her walking in the kitchen while holding onto a counter. His older sister Jean also has only one memory of their mother walking—in the living room, holding onto the wall.

Aunt Jean wanted her mom to have relationships, which at times were difficult to nurture. "I felt Mom was lonely," she says. "Her sisters were very close to her. She kept in touch with them and with an old school friend using a typewriter. She used the eraser of a pencil to type each key, which was a very slow process. These letters became 'round robins' for the sisters. Being a pastor's wife also created a natural distance for friendships, and Mom could not really take the lead in pursuing friendships. Her speech also became slurred later on, which made conversation difficult."

Why have I had a picture of Luella on my nightstand for years? Have I known somehow I have more in common with her than I first realized? I feel such a massive connection. She was not disabled at the time the photograph was taken, and her life appeared carefree. Would this snapshot look different if she would have known about her impending disability? Would she have done anything in life differently?

Multiple Sclerosis. MS. Many Scars. This refers to the scars or lesions that accumulate on nerves in the brain and spinal cord throughout the course of the autoimmune disease. Scars appear on the covering of the nerves, which is called the myelin sheath. Sometimes the scarring this disease causes is permanent, depicted by black holes on an MRI brain image. The location of scarring on the spinal cord is commensurate with the part of the body that is affected. For instance, I have scarring at the T6 level of my vertebrae, which is exactly where the numbness starts. This numbness progresses down the length of my body from that point, which is at about the middle of my chest. More prominent are the several scars on the base of my brain, the cerebellum, which mostly affects motor function, balance, and coordination. This scarring manifests itself in obvious ways in my life.

Upon receiving the multiple sclerosis diagnosis, I was suffocated by fear. Only 0.4 percent of people in the United States have the disease; just 2.3 million people in the world have multiple sclerosis. Early in this journey, when I attended a workshop regarding the three medications for MS available at that time, this fear turned to dread. A woman attending was using a wheelchair. Though I was afraid this would eventually be me, the fear faded into the background during the next eighteen years of living a life mostly unaffected by multiple sclerosis. When first diagnosed, I would regularly read the monthly publication of the National MS Society (NMSS), called Momentum. I purposely decided to stop reading this magazine within a few months because the stories of people being disabled by their disease, specifically being in a wheelchair, were not encouraging to me. Little did I know I would be in a similar position within two decades.

❝ *Little did I know I would be in a similar position within two decades.*

I wondered about the cause. Is something in my past to blame for this? Is it the long-distance running I grew to enjoy? Is it the training for the half-marathons I ran? Is it the worm carcass I found in my soda can in the late nineties? Is it because of the heat and humidity I experienced in South Texas during thirteen of my growing up years? The hot tubs I infrequently relaxed in during my early twenties? The handful of sauna trips? I will never know. Though they are actively working toward it, researchers simply don't yet know the cause of MS. Because of this inconclusiveness, there is a strong possibility I will never know, and I have to be satisfied with that.

The first eighteen years of the multiple sclerosis diagnosis were, for the most part, medically uneventful. I injected interferon once a month, alternating between injections into a quadriceps thigh muscle and a shoulder muscle. Typical for my diagnosis, I occasionally experienced dizziness. This seemed to happen during loud and exciting events, such as extended family times during holidays. My favorite hobby at the time, antique shopping, was also affected because browsing required looking from one side to another. Through the recommendation of my neurologist, and using it only as needed, I started taking meclizine, which I fondly called "dizzy pills."

Starting sporadically in the early 2000s, but increasing to frequently about five years later, I experienced double vision. My eyes seemed to see double most often when looking in the distance, particularly while driving. In 2007, a neuro-ophthalmologist suggested prisms for my glasses, for the purpose of shifting an image to where my eye wanted it to be. My vision was double horizontally and vertically. Double vision, nearsightedness, astigmatism, and the need for progressive lenses made for a complicated prescription. At that time, I wore glasses only occasionally because I typically wore contact lenses. But prisms could not be added to contacts, and I began wearing glasses with prisms ground into the lenses full-time. I currently wear very thick lenses, utilizing a combination of thirteen-and-a-half prisms for vertical and horizontal double vision. The addition of further prisms could cause the lenses to become too thick. Instead of thickening lenses, surgical tightening of the eye muscles may eventually become necessary. After this realignment of vision, more prisms could then be added.

After diagnosis, the next eighteen years were mostly physically unremarkable. I became engaged and married, had three kids, worked as a school social worker for eleven years, ran in two half-marathons, and operated an antique repurposing business. I was a stay-at-home mom, and I homeschooled my children during their preschool years. I then had the privilege of staying home during the school day, and did medical transcription through their infant, toddler, and pre-kindergarten years.

Throughout this time, I had a little numbness in the pads of the tips of my fingers, as well as the pads of my toes, but MS did not affect my everyday life at all.

I wish it would have continued in this manner. I wish it possible to learn what I have learned over the past four years without becoming disabled, but I don't think this is feasible. My faith and trust in the Lord have become deeper—I have to admit these qualities only happened because of the progression of my disease.

> " *My faith and trust in the Lord have become deeper—I have to admit these qualities only happened because of the progression of my disease.*

The NMSS, along with several other MS-focused organizations, raises an impressive amount of money geared for disease research, one of the biggest fundraiser events being the NMSS's annual bike ride, involving almost 75,000 cyclists. This and a walking event are nationally known fundraisers in which some of my friends have participated, both for my sake and simply for a challenge. Even a national donut chain joins in the publicity and advocacy.

Through these appeals for funds, the money raised is funneled into research. Though the cause of MS is still unknown, researchers diligently seek the reason for the progression of the damaging and life-changing disease. A cure has not yet been discovered, though currently there are twelve hopeful, yet outrageously expensive, medications (called Disease-Modifying Therapies or DMTs) available. Though not for the purpose of resolution or remedy, the goal of a DMT is to reduce the number and severity of MS relapses. Many pharmaceutical companies producing DMTs also offer payment assistance. The cost has the potential to make the medication unobtainable, but fortunately this has never been the case for me because of these assistance programs.

The first DMT I used, the once-a-week intramuscular injection I took for roughly seventeen years, seemed to work very well during that stage of my disease. When I hoped to become a mother, I briefly changed to a different treatment for MS that was friendlier to pregnancy. This DMT was a daily subcutaneous injection, which seemed to be more difficult to take every day, and I was very willing to switch back to my weekly intramuscular injection when this time of life was over. When more serious disease progression began, I switched to a different medication doctors hoped to be effective at the higher level of disability I was experiencing. Taking a medication that treats serious diseases can create serious side effects, which in this medication's case were cardiac. Thanks and praise go to the Lord because he has shielded me from any long-lasting difficulties with this medication or any other DMTs.

Over the past twenty-two years since my diagnosis, I have heard or read about many, many traditional and nontraditional forms of treatment, whether complementary or controversial. Well-meaning friends and even people who I have not previously known have given me articles to read, website links to research or watch, advice about alternative legal and illegal substances, and several sales pitches. Sifting through these has not been an easy task and I have gotten to the point of almost completely disregarding them.

Three times I have chosen, right or wrong, to pay attention to some of the propositions. Early in my disease, with the goal of healing, I used a "healing cloth" and prayed Bible verses about healing, a regimen prescribed by a well-known Christian healer. While this did allay my fears during this time of initial diagnosis because it taught me several Scripture verses about healing, it ended up being an attempt that didn't work for me.

Another suggestion I tried for nine months was a popular diet tailored for people with MS. The regimen included food that was gluten-free, dairy-free, and sugar-free, and the plan called for nine cups of vegetables a day. Though worth the effort, it did not make a notable difference, and it was too difficult for me to continue. Because of my increasing MS symptoms, at that point I switched to a new neurologist. My new doctor immediately made the judgment that I was "malnourished" from the diet. Because I like to eat, I was relieved to immediately call a halt to the eating plan.

Lastly, discouraged by the lack of improvement in my abilities, I went off the typical medical grid for almost a year and a half during the start of the COVID-19 pandemic. At that time, I decided to work with a naturopath since medication was not making a visible difference. This was, and continues to be, a very difficult decision. I currently have a foot in both worlds, one involves having started a new DMT when I began to need a wheelchair and the other is in the world of alternative medicine. Because of inconclusive research and opposing viewpoints from hundreds of treatment options, I constantly wonder if I am making the right decisions. I wrestle with these issues often. I never know if I am doing the right thing and I probably will always wonder.

> " *Because of inconclusive research and opposing viewpoints from hundreds of treatment options, I constantly wonder if I am making the right decisions.*

Decision-making has not been easy for me, though making them by recognizing either a feeling of peace or unrest has been critical in my life. It is one of the ways I believe the Lord speaks to me. Paying attention to the feelings the Lord gives me has led to decisions regarding complementary and alternative therapies, and I don't want to minimize his leading. In the past, these feelings of peace or unrest, marked mainly by the feeling of calmness or a pit in my stomach, have led me to make major decisions involving relationships, employment, and parenting. I have also made less consequential decisions based on these feelings, such as purchases and personal interactions.

I continually question longevity of regimens and specifics of lifestyle. Unfortunately, nothing I have tried has made a difference.

Praying to Thrive

By Debbie's dad Tom

It was a difficult day when Debbie got the diagnosis of multiple sclerosis at age twenty-five.

The good news, in addition to the outpouring of prayers, support and concern from many family members and friends, was the effect of drawing us all to the Lord God, who knows all and can do all, as he wills. In addition, Debbie's diagnosis led me back to reading about the current progress on the discovery of a cure for MS. Plus, Miriam (Debbie's mother) and I also added a specific prayer for healing from MS for Debbie, and that prayer continues today.

One memory I have is of a meeting that occurred two days after her diagnosis. It was a time of prayer I had with a friend, a man of faith who founded a company that applies Scripture to life and business principles. I told him, with some emotion, about Debbie's diagnosis and my fears for "what would happen next." This friend suggested that we go to the Healer, Jesus; he prayed "that if healing was not God's will at this time, that it would not have a negative, physical impact in Debbie's life." This is the prayer I believe God answered for the multiple years that followed!

Thus, when looking with "godly hindsight," we can be thankful for the generosity of our Lord in delaying many physical disabilities in Debbie's life. This seems to be unlike so many other MS patients, including two members of our family two generations earlier.

If I would add a Scripture passage to these years, it would be John 14:27: "Peace I leave with you; my peace I give you. I do not give to you as the world gives. Do not let your hearts be troubled and do not be afraid."

What we had prayed for about Debbie included complete healing, and then if not healing, that her condition would not worsen. The answer to this prayer changed four years ago. At that time Debbie's ability decreased so she had to use a walker, and then soon after, she used a wheelchair full-time.

While we are not able to know how these changes in Debbie's physical condition have impacted her and her family, we can observe that her attitude and perspective have been more than impressive and admirable! While it has been difficult and discouraging, I have been proud of how she and Phil have handled these changes!

These changes in Debbie's condition have reminded me of my reaction to MS in the life of my mother and my uncle (mother's younger brother). My hope and prayer are that these experiences have given me an ability to be more sensitive to the reality of MS in Debbie's life and that of her immediate family.

My mother had MS:

- She was diagnosed when I was three years old, was confined to a wheelchair within a year, and died twelve years later at age thirty-nine. Her death was not a result of MS. For almost all my youth, my mom was in a wheelchair.

- My mom was like any other mom, except she couldn't walk.

- She needed help from others (primarily Dad and we kids) for some tasks at home; and it showed we were an important part of the family when we could be of help.

- I looked forward to pushing her wheelchair when in public. I was proud to show I was her son!

- Mom's disability has made me much more sensitive to others with "specific needs" of all kinds.

- I have since realized how lonely and isolated Mom must have been and felt. She could not drive, was confined to the house, and there were no internet or cell phones.

- I was thankful for gestures of helpfulness and kindness from others toward Mom, and still today I look for ways to be of help to others with special needs.

My Uncle Roger, Mom's younger brother, was never married and lived with his parents when he returned from Korea, where he served in the Army. He was diagnosed with MS at about age thirty. He saw a continual decline in his ability to walk, and within ten years he was bedridden. Roger moved to live with his older sister, who added a room to their home for him. His condition deteriorated to total dependence, and he then lived in a care center. He died at age fifty-four.

Roger's MS life experience had an impact on me. MS treats everyone differently, even some drastically, and even those who are in the same family. MS in one member of the family impacts everyone in the family in some way. MS patients, whether family or strangers, need help, both physical and emotional, at every level of their disability. It is most helpful if the MS "patient" can express that openly. One important blessing from family and friends is them expressing care and love in personal ways and making time for special attention, largely dictated by the severity of the disease.

We can be encouraged by the Scripture passage from Isaiah 40:31 that has both present and eternal consequences for us all: "but those who hope in the LORD will renew their strength. They will soar on wings like eagles; they will run and not grow weary, they will walk and not be faint."

CHAPTER 2

The Decline

"Turn your eyes upon Jesus,
Look full in His wonderful face,
And the things of earth will grow strangely dim,
In the light of His glory and grace."

–Helen H. Lemmel, *Turn Your Eyes Upon Jesus*

June 6, 2017—a date that will be forever seared in my mind. What I had feared and dreaded during the early years of diagnosis was coming true, and I didn't know how it would end.

Grief. Loss.

More grief. More loss.

I remember walking barefoot on the wood laminate floor in our laundry room that morning and not being able to feel it completely. I slowly realized this wasn't a feeling only in the bottom of my feet, but also up and down most of the length of my legs. I was horrified to learn my body was numb from the middle of my chest down to my toes, and as the days went on, it was apparent my left side was shakier than the right. The numbness and weakness increased in severity as time went on, and the weakness continued to my upper extremities. This was the start of a slow deterioration resulting in the full-time use of a wheelchair. I call this roughly four year period of time The Decline.

During the beginning of The Decline, my legs, particularly my left leg, began to weaken. After a few months I had no choice but to start using a cane. I began physical therapy in the fall of 2018 and went intermittently for the next two years. Even though I enjoyed going to physical therapy, my condition did not improve. It only got worse. Disease progression continued, and this was very disconcerting. When I left the house in the summer of 2019, I started using a walker for the support it gave. A few months later, I used a walker all the time. Eventually using a four-wheeled walker became harder and harder, and I went to a wheelchair full-time in May 2021. This history is easy to document here, with the help of my medical journal, but experiencing The Decline was emotionally searing. Life as I knew it was over.

Life as I knew it was over.

Because of my changing needs during these difficult mobility transitions, I switched neurologists early in The Decline. It is always hard to make a doctor transition, and this was particularly difficult because I had worked with the same neurologist for roughly fifteen years. The original specialist was a very kind, grandfatherly type who had patients both with Parkinson's Disease and MS, but when The Decline began, I needed a neurologist who had expertise in MS alone. After searching, I found my current neurologist at The University of

Kansas Medical Center in Kansas City, Kansas; she researches many factors of MS and only has patients with the diagnosis.

That fateful day in the laundry room took place the summer before my youngest kids, Matthias and Laura, were about to enter kindergarten. My original intent was not to be home full-time anymore when we reached this memorable event; though I have a master's degree in social work, I did not have the intention of using it. I had loved the years of being a stay-at-home mom, but I hoped to begin to substitute teach during the week. When the school year began with my youngest two in kindergarten and oldest in third grade, I substitute taught occasionally.

My leg numbness was not obvious to anyone, and for a while, it did not affect the way I moved. But when my kindergartners came home excited to show me what they were doing in PE and expected me to copy the action, it was apparent my agility was slowed and my coordination was off. This was frustrating, and I was surprised at my lack of ability.

After all, throughout the past twenty years, I had become a long-distance runner. I got up early to run four times a week with friends. I had enjoyed training for running competitions, though I was never a serious contender; my participation was more for challenge and experience. But gradually, as my abilities slowed, runs turned into walks and then into slow walks with a cane. My running partners selflessly became walking partners and then slow walk partners. Before long, even slow walking with a cane became difficult. Through grants from the NMSS and the MS Foundation, I purchased a three-wheeled recumbent bike to use outside for exercise. After riding my modified bike for roughly nine months while my workout partners walked alongside, the long-lived early morning workout routine I had come to thoroughly enjoy was inevitably over.

As my friends continued the sessions, I remained at home. Not only did I miss the activity, I missed the regular interaction. These friends had seen me at my worst—first thing in the morning and then with sweat dripping. I felt left out, but I knew this was due to circumstance; my decision was practical and realistic. It was important for me to continue in some sort of exercise, and now I had to work out in creative ways. I needed a coach-like figure to keep me motivated because almost daily workouts required discipline, and now I had no one to keep me accountable. I soon asked a friend to do minor exercises with me, which don't even come close to the previous rigors of running or biking. We've become accustomed to seated aerobic routines, isometric exercises, and stretches.

When The Decline began, I was relieved I could still be involved in other activities I enjoyed. Because I didn't have a teaching degree, I was licensed as an emergency substitute for any age of student, pre-kindergarten through twelfth grade. As the year went on, the school hallways seemed to get longer and longer. On a day late in the school year, I was substitute teaching in a kindergarten room, and inadvertently stumbled against a student. He briefly looked questioningly at me; I was thankful no one else saw the event, because though it was extremely minor, I was embarrassed. This misstep revealed that even though subbing provided an outlet to be around people, the risks did not outweigh the benefits. The end of the year was just weeks away, and I felt terrible about running into a student. Fortunately, after this incident, I was not scheduled to substitute again because the school year was almost over. I was thankful for and relieved about the lack of substitution opportunities.

My lower body was becoming more unsteady, and the numbness increased from my chest down. I started stumbling often at home and began researching options for canes. At first, the best available option for me was a single-prong cane. A three-prong cane was eventually the most helpful and provided the support I needed. As my legs got more and more wobbly, I frequently lost my balance and even fell quite a bit. Though these falls were not a secret, I did not tell anyone if they did not witness it. Lying haphazardly on the floor was becoming commonplace.

I was frustrated with myself and the situation. Though I was relieved these falls did not cause any injuries, my irritation was growing as the falls became bothersome. My children and husband were always quick to help, but it was increasingly apparent I needed assistance with movement. Having to rely on my own decreasing arm strength to push and pull myself off the floor was sometimes not enough. I found that putting my weight on a cane was helpful, and I needed to use the support constantly; it was no longer on an occasional basis.

I had to use a cane at my oldest son Thomas' end-of-year field trip to the zoo. I was around many other parents, most of whom

I had known since our kids started school together four years before. But they didn't know I had MS. After seeing the cane, they looked questioningly at me, but didn't say or ask anything. My demeanor was unwelcoming to most questions as I had no experience fielding inquiries about my newfound struggle. It was an extremely awkward debut.

When I needed more walking support than my cane offered, towards the end of the trip I pushed a friend's stroller for stability. My friends knew what was going on and recognized the field trip was becoming difficult because of the amount of walking. They walked in a protective formation around me and helped however they could. During that zoo trip, only one other parent asked me about my use of the cane, and it happened to be another student's father. I have discovered since, in my experience and observation, it is rare for a male to ask questions about my disability. I was grateful for the chance to be frank in that short conversation as my answer was honest and straightforward. I appreciated his question and subsequent accepting demeanor. Besides experiencing his boldness and compassion, the field trip was very awkward and physically and emotionally draining.

Disappointed but not deterred, Matthias' and Laura's field trip was next. My friend Ashley remembers that day, and the difficult phone call I had to make. She said: "Debbie called me to explain her MS had started to become active. We each have a son in the same grade, and she was asking for a ride to their field trip. During this conversation she proceeded to tell me she would be bringing her cane. This had to be so hard to admit, but she handled it with such humility and courage. At this point, my heart ached for Debbie, but I was simply amazed at how she wasn't going to allow this to stop her. She was going to continue living life and not allow the MS to stop her from loving her family and spending time with her friends."

Soon after the field trip excursions, it was summer. This brought on baseball games and trips to the pool. My legs continued to get weaker. I learned quickly that the heat caused a temporary worsening of symptoms, so anything outside was not easy. On top of that, I was around even more people who had never seen me with a cane. There were lots of questioning looks and stares from people who had known me for a long time. I had lived "normally" for twenty years in the same small town. I didn't know how to deal with the wondering looks well, nor did I know what to say—most people didn't even know I had MS. Though it wasn't a secret, it had never been an issue. Because of this non-issue, I had basically only disclosed my illness to close friends. I wondered how to tell more people about the diagnosis I had received years before.

> *I didn't know how to deal with the wondering looks well, nor did I know what to say—most people didn't even know I had MS.*

In order to help handle the heat, after an application process to an MS organization, I received cooling gear created specifically for those with MS. The gear included ice packs and a vest, belt, hat, wristbands, and ankle bands designed strategically to hold them. I also purchased a stadium seat to use at kids' ball games because of a lack of core strength and the inevitable slow lean of my upper body once upright for a while. I couldn't hide my

MS even if I had tried. Wearing the cooling gear was especially obvious; it could not be disguised.

It seemed in an instant, I was disabled.

> **❝** *It seemed in an instant, I was disabled.*

This new disability was brought to public light immediately because I am not a person to stay home. My family traveled to a professional baseball game, and I decided to take a cane along. It was my first experience being anonymous and disabled in a very public place, and we hesitantly asked for tram help because of my difficulty walking. We were pleased to discover this request had a positive result—no questions were asked and there were minimal stares because no one present knew having a disability was new to me. No one there was used to me *not* needing a mobility aid: a cane, a walker, or a wheelchair. It was a relief not to juggle questions or be scrutinized by stares.

I have always wanted to use the least intrusive disability aid possible, whether it be a single-prong cane, three-pronged cane, walker, or wheelchair. The interventions I think I need do occasionally differ from others' opinions. When moving slowly in the cane stage, often my family would encourage me to use a walker when we would be going to a place that required lots of walking, such as church, shopping, or sightseeing. Whether it be pride, optimism, determination, or a sense of independence, using the least amount of mobility aid is important to me, but learning to utilize this help at the correct times has been a process. A familiar concept when previously working with special education was the requirement of Least Restrictive Environment (LRE). According to the Individuals with Disabilities Education Act (IDEA) passed in 1975, LRE means that students who are disabled should be educated as much as possible with their non-disabled peers, using the least amount of restriction possible. LRE results in students with disabilities receiving education alongside their peers without disabilities to the maximum extent appropriate.

IDEA and LRE also state that "disabled students should not be removed from the general education classroom unless learning cannot be achieved even with the use of supplementary aids and services." My personal "supplementary aids and services" are my mobility aids. I cannot be successful without them, particularly in the area of proprioception, which is the awareness of the position and movement of my body.

Though the labels depicting these realities seem to change often, the distinction is important to recognize. Using the terms disabled and handicapped can be offensive to some; it is recommended to refer to a person with these difficulties as a person who is disabled or a person with a disability. These appropriate ways of wording put the person first, and because of this, they are important to many. However, I tend to use the word "disabled" often when referring to myself. Though I certainly believe the accepted wording reflects dignity and individuality, it is challenging to keep up with the fast-changing political correctness of the phrasing.

I began to cope with many experiences which made my capability limits obvious. I started to learn how to handle these situations as I thought through every circumstance I would encounter, and I prepared any disability aids needed. I was as proactive as possible. If I was going to an outdoor event, efforts were made to sit in shade. If bleachers were the only option, I knew to sit in the first row with a stadium seat. However, most of this learning happened from making mistakes first.

I was not using a mobility aid in the late summer when my family went tent camping and boating at a nearby lake. While exploring a beach during a brief break from a boat ride, I stumbled and fell while walking through and around branches that had drifted to the shore. Looking back, I realized I should have modified my pathway in order to accommodate my walking difficulty. The least intervention needed was a cane, and I had missed the opportunity to bring it along. A few months later, this missed opportunity happened again while I was walking in brush during a darkened evening. My family of hunters was searching for a deer's dead body, as Thomas was confident of his shot. This pursuit was a difficult hike for me, and I was painfully aware of falling twice. The least restrictive mobility aid I needed at that time was a cane.

The temporary worsening of symptoms caused by heat also became more apparent, especially at places besides the pool and baseball games. Without considering the consequences, my family went for a boat ride which lasted about an hour. I sat in the full sun, not feeling hot since we were moving, and my lack of preparation became obvious. When it was time to disembark, I could not get out of the boat because of a lack of leg strength, and my husband had to lift me out. Looking back, I should have recognized the probability of my energy decreasing. Just a few months earlier, I had another experience that weakened my body. I had spent a few hours working in my flower beds, a beloved activity of mine, and, once finished and inside, I saw mainly black for a few hours. I was exhausted as I rested my splotchy vision. In general, diminished energy often led to physical tiredness, sleepiness, and the inability to talk clearly, which resulted in slurred words. It seemed I was a slow learner.

As time continued, it became increasingly apparent I needed to use mobility aids consistently, especially when I fell while inserting an extra-heavy pan into the oven. Though I didn't drop the pan, the fall resulted in dislocated ribs. I grudgingly became more realistic about my capabilities.

Summertime baseball games gave me even more opportunities to learn these mobility limits. Creating unwanted attention, I started getting rides in the city recreation director's ATV from the ballpark parking lot to the bleachers. I could not climb the bleacher stairs, and so I was dropped off to sit on the front row, where no one else sits. Because my core was no longer strong enough to keep me upright while sitting on a bleacher seat for an hour, I considered a lawn chair. But it was too hard to carry a folded lawn chair, use a cane, and keep track of three kids' water bottles, ball caps, snacks, and ball gloves while my husband was a coach and therefore unavailable. I needed help from other parents. My friends weren't always around during the game times, and I missed their selfless assistance. A few moms and dads did offer to help, but surprisingly it was rare. My sons had been playing on these sports teams for years, and the silence was disappointing at first; just a few parents asked questions. Either acquaintances didn't know what to say or my countenance continued to ward off comments. I was hoping for a friendly smile or short conversation about the game, but I learned that first I needed to make others comfortable about my situation by addressing it, though awkwardly. Despite my discomfort, it was up to me.

> **"** *I learned that first I needed to make others comfortable about my situation by addressing it, though awkwardly. Despite my discomfort, it was up to me.*

It became obvious I was tiring when my upper body started to slowly lean. This not only happened when sitting in bleachers, but was also likely when standing at a bathroom or kitchen counter. My core strength often deteriorated, and my upper body slowly leaned forward, which made it very difficult to complete needed tasks like dishwashing, handwashing, and tooth brushing. Lack of core strength also made it difficult, if not impossible, to do anything involving the simultaneous use of my arms. I became accustomed to drying my hands one hand at a time. This skill crossed over into other common tasks—styling hair, cooking, and even flossing my teeth. This lack of core strength affected me often, and the development of this glitch made time seem to slow. Menial tasks required more effort and seemed to take forever.

Later that summer, as my stamina began faltering more in the late afternoon, the addition of a four-wheeled walker was added to my mobility tools. I even used a wheelchair while on vacation in Branson, Missouri, that summer during a few activities that would require quite a bit of walking, such as Silver Dollar City, Branson Landing, miniature golf, and museums. These places were fun to explore as a family, and as a wheelchair made maneuvering easier, my children had to learn how to accompany a mother using one. This meant holding doors open, pushing the chair straight, and leaving enough space when walking next to the chair to avoid legs being inadvertently hit. Sightseeing while being at the mercy of the chair operator can be a challenge, as the length of time we each may want to spend at the site might be different. But this difficulty is worth enduring in a place where I am anonymous. As I had learned earlier in the summer, it was easier using a walking aid in a place where I didn't know anyone. This meant no wondering looks or questions and a marked decrease of awkward situations.

Back home in our small Kansas town in the fall, it was Meet the Teacher Night, which required my walker for the first time in public because of the distance between three kids' classrooms. Our beloved school was the only elementary in our very small town, and we literally knew almost everyone. At this point, I had let the teachers know what was going on, because of course we had known them for years; my husband even teaches in the same town's middle school. It was hard to get used to the many stares and questioning looks from others, though they were commonplace by now. Again, no one said anything to me. By this time, I knew that others weren't being rude or dismissive; they simply felt awkward and didn't know what to say or ask. Neither did I. Once in the comfort of my home, I sobbed for the bygone carefree walks down school halls. I knew that never again, outside of being healed, would I breeze through school visits. Never again would I carelessly move around rooms or buildings. I wept for the uncomfortable experiences I would now repeatedly encounter. Even though I never wanted to go back to the school building disabled or be in public again with my walker, the Lord gave me the strength needed to keep going with dignity, time and time again. Though my physical strength was minimal, the Lord has promised me his "power is made perfect in weakness."[1]

> " *By this time, I knew that others weren't being rude or dismissive; they simply felt awkward and didn't know what to say or ask. Neither did I.*

When school started, the elementary school carnival took place. It was outside and required lots of standing and walking, so I knew from past missteps I needed to take my walker. There were more stares and questioning looks, but yet again, no one said anything. My inner strength seemed to start waning, and I continued to grieve even more about the loss of life as I used to know it.

Then there were middle school football games later in the fall because my husband was the coach. This meant a whole new crowd of people to deal with—the middle school parents. Most did not know I had MS, nor had they even seen me with a cane, much less a walker. It was uncomfortable for all involved. This atmosphere of discomfort continued at weekly church meals. Since my husband was still at football practice when supper time started, it was easier for my children and me to go to a place where meals were provided. It was a wonderful rationale to not cook. Because I needed the amount of support it gave at the end of a day, I had to use my walker; my hesitancy was thick as I had reservations about using it for the first time in this indoor setting. I was at a loss as to how to ease myself and others into my new way of life. No one knew more than me how shocking it was for a woman in her mid-40s to have a walker, and I had grown accustomed to the questioning in the air. I decided I would have reacted in the same manner. Just a couple of years before, when I was in others' shoes, a fear of saying or doing the wrong thing also would have kept me from responding in any way at all. Unsurprisingly, the first time we attended, help seemed hard to find, but my children were amazing helpers. They seemed to be more resilient than adults, as well as quicker to adapt to change.

To prevent future questions, awkward silences, and uncomfortable feelings, I decided to make a public social media post about my MS a few days before Halloween. This decision was driven by a realization that for our small-town downtown Trick or Treat Main Street, I would need to use my wheelchair as it would be more walking than I could do successfully with a cane or walker. The use of this major disability aid had the likelihood of drawing attention, which would probably lead to noticeable stares and unspoken questions. It needed to be addressed publicly and proactively. To my relief, the overwhelming response to my candid post was quite supportive. Telling others about my disease and disability struggle was freeing and therapeutic. Now others could talk and ask questions.

I was thankful the issue had been addressed because as my legs continued to get weaker, I needed to use a four-wheeled walker frequently. In the fall, I switched to using one constantly, and I got used to lifting it in and out of the back of my van. At that time, it was a blessing to be able to walk from the driver's seat to the back hatch in order to retrieve the walker. I was determined not to let it slow me down.

At home all day without kids, I had too much time to think about my disease, and I developed a realistic fear about what the future held. The intensity of this fear seemed to come in waves, and I relied on close friends and family members to support me with their prayers during these struggles. It was helpful to have a friend's encouraging blog posted around that time. The goal of the blog was "Encouragement for everyday living"[2] and this was certainly achieved through its words of optimism about my attitude and situation. She wrote, "This journey has transitioned biblical concepts [Debbie] knew into beliefs that are engrained deep in her core—God's love and His mercy, for instance." The author concluded, "As these Truths seep deep into her bones, it has made her feel unshakable and able to stand through anything."[3]

It was imperative to rely upon this unshakable faith at my next neurology appointment. My new neurologist determined that my diagnosis had accelerated to secondary progressive multiple sclerosis (SPMS) instead of the original relapsing-remitting multiple sclerosis (RRMS). This was extremely difficult to hear because of the severity of disability associated with SPMS, but it was not a surprise. When younger, I had thought there were actually three stages of MS with the third, and worst, being Primary Progressive Multiple Sclerosis (PPMS). However, in reality, PPMS is a type of MS with persons who experience worsening disability from the time they are first diagnosed. Not being in this stage yet would have been a relief to me because it would have meant I was not at the worst stage of MS. But it was not to be so, and the determination of SPMS increased my fears of the future. This was extremely difficult news—I wanted it to go away. Instead, it stuck around. My new normal had been defined, and I didn't like it.

> **"** *My new normal had been defined, and I didn't like it.*

But according to 1 Samuel 16:7, the Lord doesn't see things the way I see them. He doesn't look at outward appearance. He looks at the heart and is interested in qualities like patience, sensitivity, and perseverance. I needed to be focused on developing these characteristics rather than having a fully-functioning nervous system. My new normal seemed unattractive, but the Lord is focused on inward appearance.

Because I was using my walker with difficulty, unsteadiness, and great slowness, sitting as much as I could throughout the day became the norm. I was even driving less frequently because my reaction abilities were slowing down. A slowing down of muscles affected my voice volume, which had probably been going on for a few years without me even realizing it. Singing had become increasingly difficult, and I needed to take breaks during times of song while in church on Sunday mornings.

I looked forward to an opportunity to have a stem cell replacement procedure in 2020. Absolute faith carried me through this procedure as I was totally convinced I would walk away from it. I spent time daydreaming about how my life would be different if I wasn't disabled at all. This meant unencumbered movement, no need for corrective lenses, regaining all I had lost—the list was endless! My hopes and assumptions left me giddy with anticipation. Obviously, I did not walk away from that strategy, and I was extremely troubled that the effort did not make a difference in my current physical abilities. Grieving and an enormous sense of loss continued.

Soon after, my entire extended family of twenty-six toured Israel. It was quite a challenge to navigate airplanes, international airports, international restaurants, Jerusalem "Old City" restaurants and stone walkways, and touring sites. Thomas, as he remembered this trip over one year later, considered traveling through airports a distinctive difficulty. It made me very thankful for the Americans with Disabilities Act (ADA) passed in 1990 by President George H.W. Bush. The ADA requires new construction to include accommodations like automatic doors, elevators, and grab bars. Also available because of ADA are ramps on street corners as well as parking for those with handicaps.

In the Holy Land, countless biblical sites were not handicap accessible. Though it was amazing to be in the same spots where Jesus and other biblical figures had been, I was extremely distracted by having to pay attention to accessibility. Nevertheless, healing was worth pursuing. Though it was not the purpose of the trip, why would I not be healed in the precise locations where Jesus walked? What about the places where he attended others' physical needs? We prayed for healing as a group at the Pool of Bethesda[4] and visited a site in Magdala that honored, among many women, the woman specified in the Gospels of Matthew, Mark, and Luke, who had hemorrhaged for quite a few years.[5] A kindly Nigerian man took my hand at the Garden Tomb to say "Bless you" after an emotional time of prayer in the possible location where Jesus came back to life. But healing was not on the agenda.

⁂

Traveling while disabled can be difficult even in the United States. When my family needs overnight lodging on vacation or on a brief trip, I must make several phone calls to inquire about accessibility. It is extremely uncommon for hotels to have wheelchair-accessible rooms that can accommodate a family of five. Traditionally they board two older adults. Rentable vacation homes are usually not possibilities because it is rare that such a home is accessible.

Occasionally it might take five to ten phone calls to find a place that fits our needs. When recently searching for trip options, it became apparent that the ease of making reservations online is over; phone calls to lodging options are now necessary. Accessibility has a different meaning wherever we go, even hotels categorize rooms differently—accommodations may be specified for those with either visual, hearing, or motor impairments. These disabilities all require different arrangements and specifications. While the phone calls may seem to be endless, it is worthwhile to ensure the destination will be safe and doable. My family's most recent trip involved an accessible room that was not as specified, as it was not the size we needed and it wasn't completely cleaned. A falling shower apparatus became the last straw, and we discovered the challenge of finding a different accessible room at the last minute. We were successful, but the experience proved I must ensure accommodations are appropriate well in advance.

Back home, my independence and ability to do things by myself began to backfire. Using my walker, I fell when attempting to go down two steps in front of the public library. Library trips had previously been weekly, but I did not go to the library for months after the public fall. Not only did I want to avoid its front sidewalk steps, I had to wait for the emotional sting to lessen.

> **"** *My independence and ability to do things by myself began to backfire.*

That fall began a path which resulted in the eventual transition to a wheelchair. The decision loomed as I had difficulty retrieving things from the floor and going up and down steps, even standing still without support. Though the use of a chair felt like a concession to my MS, I considered the situation realistically because back at our home, The Decline seemed faster and more evident. The master bedroom of our house was located in the basement with an adjoining bathroom. I had an extra walker stationed at the bottom of the stairs so I could easily maneuver downstairs. I started to descend the steps only at bedtime in order to conserve strength. I was already using a shower chair, and I started using toilet safety rails as well as grab bars strategically placed in the bathrooms. These interventions were not always successful. I fell four mornings in a row while attempting to get out of the shower; thankfully they were each slow falls and resulted in no injuries.

The fourth such incident forced me to contemplate my constantly changing new normal. After making a few attempts to right myself using the sturdy grab bars, I admitted the tub height was too high to step over, and I called out in the darkness of the early morning to my husband. The cry for help was unnecessary; he had already heard my floundering in the tub. This new habit of falling in the bathtub was a blow to my resolve, and I recognized The Decline was rapidly continuing. My bedroom and bathroom in the basement were not helping the situation, and my reluctance to make a change had the potential of danger. My husband and I moved to a ground-level bedroom in our home within a month of the bathroom falls.

Shortly after, I decided to use a wheelchair full-time. Though this was a major change in lifestyle which cannot be overstated, it was unavoidable. Wheelchair use was actually welcomed by me because the sitting alleviated my leg weakness. It was not a decision on which I dwelled or even contemplated for long; I knew it was logical. It was easier and faster for me to get around in the chair, and I knew it was the safest option.

Conveniently, a few months before the bedroom switch, we had purchased an electric wheelchair. A few years before that, a friend had given us her mother's never-used traditional wheelchair. Both are now well-utilized. I use the foldable, lightweight traditional chair as my travel chair. Inside my home, I use the heavier, rechargeable, motorized scooter full-time. It happens to be narrow and foldable as well, which makes it convenient to pack for a trip. A few years ago, before needing a wheelchair full-time, we desired something to use in locations that required plenty of walking, and at first, we thought a "transport chair" was the solution. This type of chair can only be pushed by a caregiver, instead of maneuvered by the rider, because it does not have large back wheels. But I determined this type of chair was not the best option. When pushed by another in the transport chair, I inadvertently ended up staring at museum halls and elevator walls when the operator was interested in looking elsewhere. Our hardly-used transport chair is now in storage because I quickly became frustrated with the lack of control. Though I don't have the arm strength required to wheel myself frequently, it is not a surprise I discovered I prefer to maneuver myself.

The advent of a full-time wheelchair, as well as rapid disease acceleration, made it obvious my health was continuing to decline quickly. Within a few weeks, I had a regularly scheduled teleconference with my neurologist, and she recommended five days of IV steroids. The purpose of the infusion of steroids was to decrease inflammation occurring in and around the nerves in my brain. I had five days of steroids the following week for an hour every day, and I saw an immediate difference. Having lost the ability the month before, I could now turn over in bed, get out of bed by myself, and pick my left leg up from the floor. I could move to and from the sliding, swiveling shower chair and to my wheelchair independently. Though it seemed to be a minimal difference, it was a wonderful relief to this independent soul.

My reclaimed independence was very welcome. Finally, The Decline that had lasted almost four years was over! The Decline ended with a wheelchair, but Romans 15:13 told me I would overflow with hope. Philippians 4:4 (TPT) told me to overflow with joy. I needed hope and joy! I had wondered if these qualities would automatically result from challenging experiences, but this was not true for me. They did not appear during the trial. It was obvious they were not aspects from the Lord I could conjure. Though I wished for hope and joy, and strived for them often, it was apparent I could not make them develop. I had prayerfully asked for them, and had even asked others to join me in this prayer, but I still was not joyful or hopeful. I needed the Lord's help.

He did help. One month after the end of The Decline, I became totally at peace with my current situation. This was almost four years to the day of the start of The Decline. What I had tried to achieve for four years was actually happening, even when it did not make sense—I was using a wheelchair full-time after all!

What makes sense to me doesn't matter. Blind trust does. It's moving forward without seeing the end result, while trusting everything the Lord does is good.[6]

Blind trust is discussed in 2 Corinthians 4:17-18 as an applicable understanding of peace and contentment. Accompanying "So we fix our eyes not on what is seen, but on what is unseen, since what is seen is temporary, but what is unseen is eternal" are troubles described as "light and momentary." They certainly do not seem that way! But if I trust in what I cannot see, cannot imagine, and cannot predict, my troubles do indeed become light and momentary.

Becoming content doesn't mean my grief is resolved. I still mourn for our previous way of life. "As servants of the Lord, we commend ourselves in every way...sorrowful, yet always rejoicing."[7] Even the Apostle Paul recognized sorrow and joy simultaneously; so will I.

Once again, I am supporting the world of "Big Pharma," as I have started a new medication for MS. This once-a-month injection under the skin seems harmless and easy after having injected another medicine into a muscle once a week for over fifteen years. The current DMT seems to be the direction for me to proceed at this point. Neither of the two sets of major dietary restrictions made a visible difference in The Decline. Their partial purpose was to decrease inflammation, but now it is time for me to follow the direction that medicine prescribes.

Being in a wheelchair full-time meant debuting in public for the first time. My motorized wheelchair makes it easy to ride the three blocks to downtown, allowing for the unpredictable Kansas temperature and weather. The local coffee shop was my first venture, and sure enough, I was ignored by a few casual acquaintances. It was not a surprise. No one had seen me in the wheelchair before, besides family and close friends, therefore it was a new sight to behold and uncomfortable at that. Looking back with understanding, I know now I am the one who sets the tone of social interaction. Though it is not my wish or desire to use a wheelchair, being an image-bearer of Jesus is my job in every endeavor.

> *I know now I am the one who sets the tone of social interaction. Though it is not my wish or desire to use a wheelchair, being an image-bearer of Jesus is my job in every endeavor.*

What was a surprise was the friendliness of countless shoppers a few months later at the annual downtown craft fair. The shoppers I knew personally stopped and instantly talked to me or excitedly said hello. Had I been isolating myself? Had I been on the verge of being reclusive?

When the Lord says in Isaiah 55:9 that his ways surpass the way I work, I know I can trust his ways because the word "surpass" means to exceed or to be greater than. The Lord's ways are greater than mine. I don't know why The Decline has occurred, and it certainly is not by my design, but I do know the Lord's reasoning exceeds my own. How can I not trust that? I may not like the particulars of my status, but does it prevent me from trusting in a higher good?

Questions regarding the Lord's timing lead me to probe the issue of coincidence. Does coincidence exist? Or are incidents weaving a tapestry according to the Lord's timing and purposes?

Is it a coincidence I spent eleven years working with disabled kids?

Is it a coincidence that at almost the exact same time of this disability, my husband was, and is, being called into some sort of ministry?

Is it a coincidence my husband is gifted at taking care of people? So much, in fact, that in our early years of marriage, I always thought we would be the parents of a kid with disabilities. My job experience and Phil's personality were wonderful preparation for this. I didn't realize the person with a disability would be me.

My newfound peace and contentment briefly relapsed when I had major side effects from the first injection of the new DMT. Nausea, vomiting, extreme fatigue, and dizziness briefly assailed me as I had difficulty taking deep breaths; sleep coupled with fever reducer relieved these symptoms. After a phone call to the pharmacy and medication distributor, I was reassured to discover most of these maladies were known side effects and I was encouraged to use allergy relievers and fever reducers preventively in the future. I have taken these measures, and I have not again experienced similar side effects. After the first dose reactions led to fear and worry, I immediately recognized these familiar enemies. I had a lapse in trust, but it thankfully was brief. I didn't want this complete peace I felt to be based on my circumstances. I didn't want this contentment to be like a reed swaying in the wind[8], going back and forth every which way. Contentment is an internal satisfaction which does not demand changes in external circumstances. I don't want to be upset about my external circumstances. My feelings should not be based upon the conditions which surround me.

As I entered the world of disability, how would I stay content? How would I not let my current position affect my mood? How would I handle the challenges, stares, and questions? I craved social time, so how would I invite interaction? How would I exude joy?

Sometimes well. Sometimes not so much.

Resolved to Surrender

By Debbie's mom Miriam

As I reflect on Debbie, I have feelings of absolute joy, thankfulness, and gratitude—pride in whom God made her to be. She is a model and example of someone who faces the difficult challenges of everyday life with grace and faith. Oh, that I—and all of us as followers of Jesus—would have that same trust and faith!

God has taught me many lessons in these past twenty-plus years as I've watched Debbie live with first the diagnosis and then later the reality of multiple sclerosis. These lessons have added so richly to my faith life.

First, I learned surrender. The MS diagnosis wasn't my plan for Debbie's life! I had been praying for our kids since before they were born, and this was not what I had asked God for Debbie's future. The "Mama Bear" in me came out. I was so protective of her and was upset with God and would often argue with him during my quiet time and when I walked the trail near our house: How could he possibly allow this? Why couldn't I have the MS rather than Debbie? Why didn't he heal her? I've always believed in God's healing power, so why didn't he use it now? The questions and arguments would go on. God has "big ears," and I know he listened to every complaint through those initial months of shock over the diagnosis. In hindsight, I know that he always had a plan to guide us through those tough times. I learned (actually relearned) that I don't always get my own way, that God is my daddy who knows best, that I needed to open my hands, and that I needed to let him be in charge of Debbie's life. He is faithful to all his promises! He taught me to see his goodness that is so evident in my life! Circumstances aren't always necessarily good, like living in a wheelchair as Debbie currently does, but God is definitely good each and every day.

I also learned the fact of his goodness. I have seen God's fingerprints throughout my life, and it would take a book to contain all those stories! But as I reflect on his goodness in this part of my story, being Debbie's mom during the years of her MS, I realize how he has grown my trust and faith as a result of all she has gone through. God has opened my heart to others who have unique needs. Although I don't think of Debbie as being disabled—she is simply my daughter whom I deeply love—I now have more awareness of those who have special needs and I have a desire to connect with them so they know they are seen and that someone cares. That is not me, it is God working in me. He is growing me to look more like him in large part because of Debbie's influence in my life.

The lesson of God's goodness has helped teach me gratefulness to God for his daily blessings that have been more than I could ask or imagine. And one of those is Debbie. I am so grateful for the gift she is in my life and for the way she has faced her MS challenge. Her focus on being positive has greatly influenced me to *not* dwell on what she can't do but on what she can do: Being the amazing wife and mom that God called her to be, being a faithful and faith-filled friend to many, and being an "influencer" for both family and friends. I'm also incredibly grateful to God for Phil who exhibits the same faith qualities as Debbie and demonstrates his commitment to her and the kids consistently. And speaking of the kids, I'm so grateful they are learning to "step up" and serve as the needs arise. I'm proud of all the family! In my mind right now, I'm thinking of an unending list of reasons to be grateful, but one in particular is their small-town community, and all the friends who in the past and still today are walking alongside the Oelke family and helping in many wonderful ways.

One of the most important aspects of my life is the prayer-heart God has grown in me, which is directly connected to Debbie's MS story. I grew up only knowing memorized prayers—and I'm not being critical of that because I know that particular kind of praying was how my parents were raised. But through the years of my husband Tom's ministry and being active in church life, God taught me how to pray "from the heart." He grew that heart in me and made it a priority in my life, for which I am forever grateful. In the years Debbie was growing up, God was preparing me for the time in my life when she was diagnosed. Her MS situation, even though symptoms were mild in the beginning years, increased my time devoted to prayer, which in turn greatly enriched my entire prayer life. It led me to reach out to others. Soon through Bible study friends, through family (both immediate and extended), through friends in our previous churches, through prayer chains all over the country and even around the world, God grew a huge army of prayer warriors who were pouring out their hearts to our Father's throne on Debbie's behalf. And now, more than twenty years later, many are still praying for her. The prayers kicked into high gear a few years ago when the symptoms became more obvious and made life more difficult for Debbie. I'm so thankful for this praying army which never gives up hope. They have been a huge blessing and

I have had a lasting lesson on persistence in prayer. This is one of the beautiful ways I see God's fingerprints on my life.

And those fingerprints are still obvious. God has done amazing things in Debbie's life and continues today. Many years ago at her confirmation when she was thirteen, Debbie picked out a special Scripture – Psalm 27:1 (KJV): The LORD is my light and my salvation; whom shall I fear? The LORD is the stronghold of my life; of whom shall I be afraid?

Debbie lives and models that verse every day of her life. To God be the glory, great things he has done!

CHAPTER 3

On Being Disabled

"Abide with me, fast falls the eventide
The darkness deepens Lord, with me abide
When other helpers fail and comforts flee
Help of the helpless, oh, abide with me."

–William Henry Monk, *Abide With Me*

How sudden is sudden?

All of a sudden, within the span of four years, I am a disabled person. In the scheme of forty-seven years, four years doesn't seem sudden. It's less than one-tenth of my life. Becoming disabled was not immediate. Though The Decline seemed instantaneous, it was a slow downhill progression.

But it was completely unprecedented and unexpected. It was unwanted and unbecoming. It was despised and disruptive. It created dismay and disorder.

Disabled means limited in movements, senses, or activities. To make inoperative or ineffective. A thesaurus search suggests the words deactivate, defuse, or disarm. I certainly don't feel like I am rendered useless, as these definitions seem to suggest.

The Latin prefix dis has a negative or opposite definition, which results in "disable" meaning "not able." I am not able to do lots of things; in fact, it seems I am not able to do almost anything. Or I do things very differently. I keep saying, "That's something I could never do in the past," when discussing actions like turning cartwheels, running a marathon, or swimming the butterfly stroke. It seems strange that I had the ability to attempt those things at some point. It probably sounds especially odd to my kids, who cannot remember a time when I wasn't disabled. It probably sounds especially odd to a person who may not realize I was not disabled for 43 years. But I may not ever have the opportunity to try those things again. Such is the reality of being disabled.

> **"** *But it was completely unprecedented and unexpected. It was unwanted and unbecoming. It was despised and disruptive. It created dismay and disorder.*

Becoming disabled is as if I am wearing a different pair of glasses. Anyone who wears corrective lenses knows adjustment to a new prescription takes a while. As new lenses can initially make one dizzy and then feel as if one is looking with eyes wide open, disability initially causes negative feelings, and it has opened my eyes wide to a completely new-to-me world.

I am newly seeing the world around me with each additional stage of disability. Literally, my views from a floor and bathtub, as well as from a consistent four feet while sitting in a wheelchair, show an unusual aspect. Observing contexts from my disabled lens, I am not as quick to judge others or make assumptions.

I am now part of the largest percentage, 29.7 percent, of those receiving disability income benefits (Social Security Disability Income—SSDI). This greatest portion includes those who suffer from disability of the musculoskeletal system and connective tissue, and multiple sclerosis fits this category. MS conditions allow for benefits because of how much the diagnosis can impact everyday life, such as making it nearly impossible to work. Everyday life also includes interactions with loved ones.

Before I was married at the age of twenty-seven, I spent lots of time with built-in friends, my three siblings. As we got older, this included their spouses, which resulted in six brothers and sisters, all close in age. We love to remember family times—vacations, various sports played together, dance clubs, church camps, visits to grandparents' houses, holidays, and being pastor's children together. It probably sounds strange to their younger kids, my nieces and nephews, to hear us talk about times when I was walking unimpeded because most of them also cannot remember a time I was not disabled. I love rehashing these stories, especially because I had the ability to walk, run, dance, and jump in them. The embarrassing moments were indeed numerous, but we have many priceless memories of our growing up and adult years. This reminiscing seems to be important to my siblings as well. My older brother Tim shares, "I have found myself wanting to hold onto the memories of Debbie's younger years more tightly. I want to remember those times of her active lifestyle, running track, leaping over tennis nets, cheerleading, etc., to relish in those memories, and to smile because of them. It feels somewhat surreal, like in a dream. I find myself wondering, 'Is this really the situation now?'"

> **"** *Is this really the situation now?*

Subsequently, the first time I was in a wheelchair around my siblings, their spouses, and their children was extremely difficult. To see someone roughly every four months and have them go backward in their physical abilities quickly during that time of absence can seem like the decline was especially sudden. My siblings are, understandably, disturbed by my disability, as of course are my parents. All have offered to help however possible. Being very willing to push my wheelchair, hold me steady when standing, or carry any necessary supplies without me asking is an indication of their love and concern. Our closeness is evident. Without speaking about it, they are committed to treating me as they always have. Sitting around our parents' kitchen table in the early morning with our open Bibles in front of us is a mental souvenir of family gatherings. Remembering old times, going for neighborhood walks, playing card or board games, and helping with meals together will always be some of my most cherished family times. Tim adds, "In addition to sadness, it has also created a thankfulness inside of me. A gratitude for what is given and to just try to enjoy the moment we are in as much as possible."

When in college, my twin sister Beth and I would occasionally visit Tim at the university he attended in a different state. During one of those stays, I met a young man who was in a wheelchair. I was amazed at his ability to dance while in the chair—he expertly moved it rhythmically and skillfully. I was very impressed with him at the time and am even more so now, almost thirty years later. That young man seemed to thoroughly enjoy life despite his handicap.

I want the next generation of my extended family to arrive at the same conclusion. With my nieces and nephews, I can take pleasure in my surroundings and continue to eat out, go shopping, get pedicures, or cheer them on at athletic events. We can still play card games, work on puzzles, and read books together. I can provide motorized wheelchair rides to the youngest family members who enjoy them just as much as my own children. My siblings' ingrained habit of serving others is evident in their children—the next generation doesn't hesitate to make accommodations for me.

My younger brother Matt and I share a special bond as the two "babies" of the family. He said he has wrestled through many stages of grief when it comes to my disease, including denial. "At first, I didn't want to hear any details because that would mean it was real," he shared. Another of his emotions has been guilt, wondering why I was given this to bear and not him.

Matt's progression through grief at this point has landed at anger. Since denial is hardly an option anymore when he sees me using mobility aids, he said he has "almost a fighting theme" to his attitude. "Where in the past I may have not wanted to hear the details, now with the anger I have towards her condition, I want to fight it for her. I believe seeing her faith and attitude the past few years have helped me change how I am affected. She's living it and has a better attitude than I have. That has helped me open my eyes more and want to come alongside her and fight. I just don't know how...I feel helpless, but want nothing more than her healing."

⟨⟨⟨⟨⟩

Beth, who is my identical twin, does not have MS. Thankfully, she has only a thirty percent chance of developing it. If MS were completely genetic, then Beth would have a 100 percent chance of having it, because both of us have exactly the same genes. Most scientists agree that our DNA is 100 percent similar, but new studies show there can be mutations. In fact, an estimated fifteen percent of identical twin pairs may have one member that exhibits major genetic variation from their twin. I am that twin who exhibits major variation. Though Beth and I are passionately independent and enjoy diverging from popular culture, this type of variation is unwanted.

I am filled with relief Beth does not have MS. This is a blessing that we recognize as an act of the Lord. Thankfully, MS is not completely genetic, but because the diagnosis has a "genetic predisposition," there is increased risk, and there will always be cause for concern.

Unrelated to MS, Beth had an MRI roughly fifteen years ago because parts of one of her arms were numb. Her doctor could not pinpoint a cause of the numbness, besides carrying her baby son in that arm, but he recommended an MRI be done to gather additional information. An unintended bonus was that this MRI showed no concerns about MS, and the numbness went away eventually. Beth shared she still has numbness in both arms when she uses them quite a bit, and she credits this to carpal tunnel syndrome. It is not a coincidence I have had this same condition, for which we both have been surgically treated.

Having an identical twin sister unaffected by multiple sclerosis is definitely a bright point along this journey. I harbor no ill will, and from my standpoint, there have never been questions of "Why me?" But I know Beth experiences guilty feelings over my ongoing disability and her good health. Though she lives farther away than I would prefer, our relationship has taken on a different dimension during The Decline. Not needing to say a word, I can call her and simply cry. She is likely to be extremely overprotective, for which I am thankful—she is older than me, after all, even if it is just by five minutes. No matter my disability, we have been, always are, and will continue to be unwavering supports for each other.

> " *There have never been questions of "Why me?"*

Beth and I love to shop together, and this love has easily transferred to some of my friendships. This hobby has changed in manner since being in a wheelchair. Antique shopping, a previous staple, is now almost impossible because these stores often have aisles which are too narrow for a wheelchair or they require weaving in and out of merchandise. Shopping in a place where I am around people I know can be awkward, whether it's college friends or hometown acquaintances. Shopping does not seem to lend to the seriousness of a conversation about disease and disability, which contributes to brief floundering remarks.

Beth and I are no longer together as often as we would like. But when we are together in public, we are often asked if we are sisters or even twins. Since becoming disabled, I have noticed this doesn't happen as much, and when we take photographs together now, it is with sadness and nostalgia I see the differences between us. We no longer look as alike as in the past since I use disability aids and wear glasses; however, during a recent weekend shopping trip, it was to my pleasant surprise that we were asked twice about being twins. Perhaps this recognition shows others respond well to the normalization of my disability.

When shopping, I need to view circumstances from all angles. A simple store errand is now very different; stairs are noted and elevators are necessary. Whether it's Beth partially trying potential clothes on for me in a shopping aisle because of COVID-19 closing down the dressing room, or my daughter pushing my wheelchair to endless public bathrooms, we try to transform any potential obstacles into fun. Strangers have helped us reframe potentially unpleasant experiences— whether it is a woman graciously smiling when accidentally backing into her in a store aisle or countless shoppers getting out of the way when I steer into their lanes, I note others' acts of kindness!

Just as Beth claims I'm the one who tends to initiate conversation with others when we are out in public together, I'm now also relied upon to normalize wheelchair use. I'm counted on to act and talk as if my current situation is natural.

The ease with which we now speak to others has not always been the case, however. Throughout high school, we were both painfully shy; being reserved in social situations made parts of growing up difficult. I hoped I wouldn't be quiet the rest of my life, and though I would describe myself as partially introverted, I am more talkative now. In fact, neither of us would consider ourselves reserved anymore. Therefore, initiating or maintaining conversations is not a hardship for me now, and I have no problem assuming this role. I credit this ease to the Lord. He used a summer job during college to teach me how to introduce myself constantly to various storekeepers, as well as engage them in conversation. During my college years, I was relieved to grow out of my shyness. I became a person who exhibited confidence and comfort in herself.

However, having conversations with others has changed in part. Talking with others now depends upon my ability to move around, and most often, conversing is conditional upon others approaching me. Because of previously teaching social skills as a school social worker, including the finer points of having a conversation—initiating, maintaining, and ending them—I am acutely aware that my social interactions no longer seem to rely on me. I depend on others for these intricacies. It makes me wonder if I have become less talkative in social situations. In settings where I barely know others and am not able to initiate interaction, I probably do become less involved. This setting is uncomfortable for me because I enjoy being able to interact. If I can help it, I like to stick around after an event to converse, but my chair is usually in the hands of another. I am not always the one in control of my movement, the location I go, or the direction I face.

> *Talking with others now depends upon my ability to move around, and most often, conversing is conditional upon others approaching me.*

Recalling the public debut of my first walking aid, a cane, is clear. Although many of these thoughts bring back difficult memories, it seems like the use of a cane was easier than a wheelchair.

At least with a cane I could still reach everything I wanted.

At least with a cane I could go every place I desired.

But then moving to a walker during the first years of The Decline limited me more, particularly when reaching out, over, up, or down. It also took longer to get places, as I had to lift the walker in and out of the back of my van. One of these times, upon arriving at a friend's house, I fell while trying to get my walker out of my van when parked on a slope. Though I was embarrassed about the public fall, I appreciated the onlooking friends' and witnesses' reactions. While some took immediate charge of the situation by devising a plan to get me into the house, others made themselves available while asking how I wanted to proceed. Both types of interaction were appreciated, but I ended up riding on my walker's seat to the front door while being pushed. I learned that while most people are very willing to give assistance, some prefer to be told exactly what to do.

The friends who were present that day had never seen me grieve about my disability. When I returned to my van, I certainly did so. The primary person there who helped me get back to my vehicle when the event was over was full of encouragement, a comfort I needed to hear. Since this occasion, I have come to better know and understand her own challenges in life. Did my authenticity encourage her to be honest and real about her own difficulties? Agreeing with another that life sometimes has adverse situations seems to create a bond.

As time passed, getting up and down stairs became more difficult for me, and I navigated ADA ramps for the first time. I discovered a usable ramp is often farther away from building entrances, which does not bode well for easily tired legs. In the past, I occasionally chose to avoid ramps and climb stairs instead, but I reconsidered this decision when I fell again when using my walker on steps. I resigned myself to forego stairs and alternatively use ramps; the truth of the matter was disappointing.

Moving into a wheelchair limited my capabilities even more, though it is actually a relief, physically, for me to sit. It affects all I do. Life appears to be in slow motion because it takes longer to do everything. Every. Single. Thing. It prevents me from leaving the house as often as I would like. It prevents me from driving a vehicle regularly, and it prevents me from going anywhere by myself. I always need someone to help me when I arrive at my destination. I consistently need assistance by having someone lift my wheelchair out of the van, bring it to my door, and then push it. Drive-through banks, pharmacies, and restaurants are helpful and appreciated. Grocery store pick-ups are seamless to navigate. While full-service gas stations are of the past and an undervalued convenience, my small Kansas town happens to have one such locale. This station is a must for me.

> " *Life appears to be in slow motion because it takes longer to do everything. Every. Single. Thing.*

Even small daily tasks are affected by being in a wheelchair. For example, how to navigate the height of everything, such as the sink, has become an issue. I now brush my teeth completely differently than in the past. Getting clothes from a closet or dresser, getting in and out of bed, getting dishes in and out of the cupboard, retrieving food out of the fridge, making coffee, and filling my glass from the sink have all been specifics I have had to figure out. I've completely changed the location of applying makeup and styling hair, as well as the position of using my computer and eating a meal. It takes longer, even twice as long or more, to do things like bathe, get ready in the morning, and prepare food.

Because I sit all day now, I especially find myself continuing to care for my physical appearance. I still have some control of how I look. However, I have no control over the occasional slurring of my words when tired. I have no control over my low voice volume because of weakened voice box muscles. Having a quiet voice is frustrating to me. What I hear in my mind seems to be loud enough. However, after being asked countless times to repeat myself, I am aware I need to increase the volume I speak with. But, in my mind, it sounds as if I am yelling.

Noise heard in my head and the actual output is a balance to reconcile, and I most often default to using a low amount of volume in order to not seem like I'm yelling.

Each mobility aid has affected all these various details of life, as well as many church-related activities. When I used a cane, I wondered if I should have knelt for Communion. Should I have even left my seat for the sacrament when using a walker? Navigating a cemetery because of uneven ground was difficult with either device, as was the possibility of going up a few stairs at church in order to make an announcement, participate in a family Advent candle-lighting ceremony, or be a part of a missionary commissioning. I wondered if I should attempt these activities or if it was better to let someone else do them. It has become a moot issue. Because my husband, Phil, and I have been led to gather others in our home for a "house church," we no longer attend an organized church.

When I have arrived at church activities with a different form of mobility aid throughout the last four years, first with a cane, then a walker, and now a wheelchair, I have experienced everything I encounter in any other public situation. Those who follow Jesus also stare, don't know what to say, or unintentionally say the wrong things. Undertaking the challenge to ignore the obvious is similar to not paying attention to an unreasonable toddler screaming in a public situation. Trying not to look at the toddler and the parents can be difficult. However, I have appreciated when others attempt ignoring, behaving as if he or she is unaffected by being around something different. Being disabled is hard enough.

Being disabled is hard enough.

Attending concerts, seminars, and shows, as well as searching for accessible seats, can be complicated. Sometimes I avoid these events because of the inconvenience of restroom location and parking. Such venues often locate wheelchair seating in the back row or together in an area that's not conducive for children. For these accessibility reasons, I must consider each event separately. Will I attend friends' or family graduations, weddings, funerals, receptions, and other such events? Will my husband be available to accompany me? If not, will one of my children? A friend? Extended family? Someone I hardly know? Nevertheless, when Matthias and Laura had a choral performance, I relied upon an acquaintance to open a heavy restroom door. It confirmed my belief that others are very willing to help, and they are most gracious about the assistance.

Being in a wheelchair often affects where I sit in a room. Every time I wheel to a room in my own house or others', I consider whether I should stay in my wheelchair or transfer to a more comfortable seat. While it is one more step to transfer, once I do so, I feel the same as everyone else. Though I have only used this wheelchair for nine months, my body, especially my back, sometimes resists the never-ending pressure. It often, prematurely, has had enough of the constant sitting.

Because of being wheelchair-bound, I can no longer jump on the trampoline, play outdoor games, or eat outside with my children. I cannot even help to get balls out of trees or climb the attic stairs. Ascending into the attic, though hot and dark, used to be exciting; now I miss the adventure. While I would like to retrieve extra tables, Christmas decorations, or camping equipment by myself, I now must rely on others' timing.

I even question the potential of holidays spent at relatives' homes. Our extended families do what is necessary for us to spend a weekend with them, which is extremely gracious, but it is always a relief to be home and utilize familiar conveniences. The distance of grab bars, width of doorways, and number of stairs are concerns and can be a safety issue. To say my husband, kids, extended family, and friends are wonderful and very willing to help with transportation transitions is both humbling and a huge understatement.

Being disabled does have some bright sides.

I have to acknowledge that parking closely because of a handicapped placard that hangs from my rearview mirror is wonderful.

Also helpful is using a swiveling, sliding shower chair.

Earlier in The Decline, I relished using a motorized scooter at big box stores, though the loud, incessant beeping when in reverse is a deterrent.

In the cane and walker stages, I had gotten to ride in the local recreation director's ATV to ball games from my parking spot.

It is an obvious advantage that I get to sit out of dog poop picking-up parties in the backyard.

> **"** *It is an obvious advantage that I get to sit out of dog poop picking-up parties in the backyard.*

I have the privilege of a woman coming to my house for five or six hours a week to do all of the cleaning and laundry.

We enjoy the blessing of organized meals prepared and delivered by friends and acquaintances once or twice a week. It seems to be the only instance in which our meals include vegetables, and we anticipate the varied weekly menu. Our family also appreciates the use of paper plates and getting to eat frequent dessert. In addition, generous townspeople and coworkers keep our freezer stocked with meals.

We have much to praise the Lord for!

Because my mobility is similar to those about thirty years older than me, I connect well with that age group. In the past, pre-Decline, I very wrongly assumed this population was mentally deficient. Therefore, I would converse loudly, simply, and slowly with them. I have discovered that because of my wheelchair, others who don't know me have this same assumption. It seems they think because I have a physical disability, I must have a mental loss as well. Though this is bothersome to me, it is exactly what I've presumed about others in the past.

This belief began in my growing up years in Galveston, Texas. My siblings and I would sometimes accompany our father and mother on hospital calls. We often visited a man with quadriplegia who lived his entire adult life in a hospital bed. I distinctly remember the dedication of his wife; I also recall my almost-fearful feeling of looking at his bald head, scaly skin, and unmoving hands. I gladly watched the television, as it was an entertaining distraction. At the time, my assumption was that he lacked mental clarity, but in reality, this incorrect belief was most likely caused by my discomfort and sadness regarding the situation.

I have now been in a similar position. When in public, strangers tend to talk to those who accompany me instead of addressing me directly. Possibly they assume that I do not have mental clarity. A friend has stated I need a hat reading "I'm With It." This is laughingly true. But is it funny if I actually see the value of wearing such a hat? I get tired of being treated as if I'm of less importance. Being ignored is wearisome.

When I volunteered for our elementary school book fair, the students assumed I was alert because they had lots of book paraphernalia questions for me. It seemed to be a successful attempt at normalizing disability.

This normalization was opposed to the middle school and high school fundraiser two weeks before. Paying adults bypassed me as I sat with an open cash box on the table directly in front of me. Instead, they asked the person next to me where payment was taken. Wasn't it obvious? Why else would I be sitting there with money out? I was angry, and it was certainly okay to experience that feeling. We can look at Jesus's example.[1] But he had good reason. Did I? He has told me to extend forgiveness.[2]

Had I? I expected others to have a demeanor that accepted everyone and everything. But did I? Do you?

> " *I expected others to have a demeanor that accepted everyone and everything. But did I? Do you?*

I was learning my disability was easier for children to handle than adults. We adults are used to our routines and interactions. Because of these habits, those who are disabled are often isolated or left out. A new goal of mine, still unobtained fully, is to talk to anyone using mobility aids, particularly a walker or a wheelchair, because the people using them are almost always alone, seemingly in a corner. Not being talked to. Even I, a person who is disabled yet outgoing, don't always know what to say. I do not want to fall into the trap of saying something only to avoid the awkwardness of silence or of saying something that is hurtful or insensitive.

People with disabilities make up the United States' largest minority at almost fifty million strong, just about twenty percent of the population. One in five people in the United States are affected by a disability. The popularity of the every-four-years Paralympics is on the rise. At the 2021 Paralympics in Tokyo, there were over 4,500 athletes representing more than 160 nations. American athletes at this event are starting to get opportunities for endorsements. The current push is to change the language from a *disabled* sport to an *adaptive* sport. Those of us with disabilities should advocate for our needs, as this minority presents challenges to the nondisabled person. Among these challenges is being able to acknowledge differences and accept them.

These differences are evident in products available for those who need adaptive items. My husband and I visited a medical supply store, and we were impressed with the sheer volume of materials for people with disabilities. I noticed advocacy and acknowledgement immediately. I had never been in a store like that before, and if it were closer, I would shop there regularly. Who knew there are bed rails, safety bars, shower chair baskets, and walker accessories available? What about silverware extensions, extra-long grabbers, and wheelchair headlights?

These advantages would help to increase activities of those with disabilities, because those with disabilities seem to not be in public often. Is the reason because public places usually prevent a disabled person from being part of the crowd? For instance, does anyone consider that bleachers are difficult to navigate and the placement of bathrooms is often too far away? Do architects notice a lack of ramps and the sometimes distant location of accessible parking options make attendance a challenge?

Parking lots, stairs, ramps, and public toilets must be considered each time I leave the house. The placement of these can be a challenge. I debate whether it is even worth attending events because of the difficulties that might be presented. Bathrooms, private or public, are particularly convoluted to navigate in a wheelchair, and sometimes even difficult to find. My father remembers being embarrassed for his mother when she and her family were traveling and needed to find a restroom. When they did, my grandfather took her to one that was available, which, my father now speculates, was probably awkward. My Aunt

Jean also has a sixty-year-old memory related to bathrooms. She says, "We traveled [and] I had to check the bathrooms to see that no one was in there. [I] then 'stood guard' to make sure no one would enter when Dad was helping Mom. I hated doing that, yet I truly understood the importance of my job."

> **❝** *Parking lots, stairs, ramps, and public toilets must be considered each time I leave the house.*

Small, handicap-accessible, public restroom stall size can sometimes be a difficult space in which to maneuver. A stall might be large enough to hold a wheelchair, but that doesn't mean it's big enough to turn the wheelchair around in it. Footrests make it even more challenging. Having experienced an occasional loss of dignity because of these issues, my family and I are quite aware of correct ADA implementation. Sometimes even accommodating restroom stall doors can't close when they're not large enough to fit a wheelchair. When this happens, which is often, I have been forced to leave my chair outside the stall and walk inside it, heavily relying on others for assistance, if not Laura, a friend, Beth, or my mother. I once reached for inappropriately placed grab bars—it resulted in falling and sliding on the floor of a stall. Kindly, a woman in the neighboring stall caught glimpses of the bumbling and asked if I needed assistance. Help and strength from the Lord has quickly been requested in numerous similar situations; he gave me exactly what I needed to stand during this awkward mishap.

It is important and beneficial for me to proactively pay attention to restrooms in private homes, hotel rooms, restaurants, and convention centers. It is to my advantage to ask if a location is accessible. Parking is also an issue, and there are conspicuous differences between parking efficiently while using a cane, walker, or wheelchair. When using a walker or wheelchair, if a handicapped parking space is half a block away from a ramp utilized to get onto the sidewalk, this occasionally renders as pointless a closer handicapped parking place. It is easier and more efficient for me to park in a regular space as near to the ramp as possible. Therefore, there are times I don't even use handicapped parking because it does not make arrival more convenient. When using a wheelchair, however, whether it is raining or not, using handicapped parking which is "van accessible" is helpful because my wheelchair can be maneuvered right up to my door.

Ramps can be a determining factor in other locations. Aquatic therapy, stemming from physical therapy, has been recommended for me at various times throughout The Decline. There happens to be an indoor pool at a neighboring town fifteen miles away, but the ADA ramps present a dilemma. I have to decide every time I attend whether to use a walker or a wheelchair on the outdoor ramp and the indoor ramp that enters the pool itself. The distance of the start of the indoor ramp from the outside door is an issue, and the ease differs depending on the mobility aid. If I were to go now, I would need a waterproof wheelchair. Though I have loved aquatic therapy exercises in the past as part of my treatment, the accessibility aspect prevents me from taking advantage of it now.

Having toured in Israel while in a wheelchair and either navigated, or chosen not to navigate, tunnels, steps, narrow doorways, restrooms, airports, and cobblestone sidewalks and streets, I am especially appreciative of the ADA in the United States. In Jerusalem, I waited patiently while my family members waded through Hezekiah's Tunnel, built during the king's reign in 700 BC to redirect water. At Wadi Qelt, I read Psalm 23 on the tour bus while everyone else climbed a hill to see the assumed Valley of the Shadow of Death. In the village of Bethany, I remained in a side street while they climbed down steps to Lazarus' tomb. In the home of Caiaphas, high priest and leader of the ruling council in Jesus' time, I peered down through a window to see where Jesus was imprisoned the night before his death. I was truly thankful my husband, kids, siblings, parents, and nieces and nephews were able to experience each of these sites. They are important pieces of biblical history, but the inability to access them was frustrating. Appreciative of the time Phil and I toured many of the same sites fifteen years earlier, I focused on remembering significances, sights, and memories of the past.

At a recent middle school football game, a friend of Matthias' said to him, "No offense, but is your mom in a wheelchair?" Matthias then asked me if it indeed was offensive, to which I replied, "No, this is life for us!" We can be real about life with a wheelchair, and we should normalize our way of life. We can choose not to be offended or embarrassed about it. Matthias said this is the first time he was asked this, but I wish others had the courage to ask questions like this nine-year-old.

> **"** *We can be real about life with a wheelchair, and we should normalize our way of life.*

Courage is required in many of life's circumstances. To deal with aspects of different seasons and manage them is not easy, but the Lord wants us to learn something from these situations. He can turn absolutely anything around for good. Though The Decline has been a sudden and seemingly quick progression of disability, I have had four years to grasp the Lord's purposes through it.

The Lord comforts me in Isaiah 61:3 by saying he will make beauty from ashes and give me "a garment of praise instead of a spirit of despair." My feelings of despair *should* turn to praise! It is hard for me to praise the Lord while consistently seeing life from an almost four-foot-high perspective, though. From my point of view, I can more easily see every mark, dent, or scrape I have made with my wheelchair on walls and furniture, especially on doorways that aren't wide enough. Frustratingly, I can also easily see the two holes I have made in my home's drywall, each dented with either my van or my wheelchair. A large crack in the water bottle holder attached to my motorized wheelchair is a nuisance that reminds me daily of my "demolition derbies"— my clumsy attempts at movement, appropriately nicknamed by my kids. It is tempting to despair because of these issues. Praising the Lord doesn't always come naturally.

But praise the Lord I have three children! As all do, my own kids love comparing their height to mine. I enjoy standing up during these times, mostly because they are still shorter than my five-foot, four-inch frame. Making this determination while standing, rather than sitting, is more meaningful since this is how we did it before I sat in a wheelchair all day. I absolutely want to stand for these unofficial determinations now.

Being a wife and mother obviously means much to me, as do my relationships with others and especially with the Lord. Though I want to be considered the same as I always have been and as "normal," I have to decide what "normal" means for me now. I have to consider how this normal affects the way I desire to be treated.

Determined to Rejoice

By Debbie's sister Beth

Watching my sister become disabled has been one of the most emotionally difficult times of my life, which seems ridiculous to even say. She is the one who has lost mobility and is now unable to do so many things physically that she used to love to do. All I've done is sit on the sideline and watch, but it has been hard for me as her twin, sister, and best friend.

I'll never forget when Debbie was first diagnosed about twenty-five years ago. She had gone through a two-year-long process of doctor visits to try to find an explanation for symptoms she was experiencing, so when a diagnosis finally came, it was quite welcome. However, it was also devastating all at the same time.

Debbie was living in a small Kansas town at the time, and I was living over two hours away in the Kansas City area. Debbie called to share the diagnosis with me, and I jumped in the car immediately to be with her. I remember crying the entire drive there, and when I got out of the car, she greeted me with the question, "Did you cry the whole way here?" I laughed and replied, "Of course I did." And now reflecting on that conversation, it is exactly how we have handled her disability ever since: with humor and directness and tears. There has been laughter over hitting other people or sidewalk cracks with her wheelchair. There have been very direct conversations about having children and what the future holds. And there have been countless phone calls where no words have been spoken, yet many tears have been shed.

To me, there is no more helpless feeling than watching someone you love suffer physically and being unable to help. This is compounded by the fact that Debbie and I live five hours away from each other now and have our own families, so simply jumping in the car to visit is not an option.

When Debbie first began to lose the ability to walk several years ago, I did not know what to do or how to help, so I made the decision to just start buying things that would be delivered to her. I sent her all kinds of gifts, about half of which she probably truly wondered about. I called her more frequently. My mom and I discussed her on a weekly basis. I found ways to buy even more things for her. I prayed for her. I asked friends to pray for her. And, of course, I cried.

Debbie's situation became even more real when we did spend time together. The first time I witnessed her using a cane was at a party following the adoption of my youngest son. She needed to walk from the back door out onto the back porch, down the steps, and across the grass to a table. She used a cane for this and clearly struggled with it. One of the next experiences we had together was traveling to Texas for a craft fair. She used a motorized scooter, which was extremely helpful. This made shopping at the fair a unique experience, yet I was thankful we had a way to do it successfully and somewhat easily for Debbie's sake. I don't think we will ever forget having to eat blueberries that were squished by me hanging the bag right next to her scooter wheel.

Probably my favorite experiences in recent years have been clothes shopping with Debbie in a wheelchair. Getting her wheelchair in and out of the car successfully is an art in itself (and easier if it is not raining), and then managing to navigate parking lots, ramps, doorways, and sidewalks is another challenge. Debbie and I both get motion sickness easily, so it is especially challenging to steer and handle her wheelchair in such a way that she does not feel sick. Thankfully, she does take "dizzy pills" here and there! Then, when we finally get in the store, I get to help pull clothes from the rack to show her, and I even get to try clothes on and model them for her. Thankfully, we have always been about the same size, so this is no problem. During COVID-19, it was a bit challenging though, since most dressing rooms were closed. We solved this problem by having me try on shirts right over my clothes in the aisle. We always enjoy shopping together. We give each other honest feedback and usually fall in love with the same things!

I have to admit I have had guilt over living my life normally while my sister struggles so much. It's embarrassing to admit I did not tell her I was training for a half-marathon until the race was about to occur. I also rarely tell her when I do other favorite physically active things I know she no longer does, such as kayaking, traveling, walking around our property, hiking, or running. When Debbie was first diagnosed, she stopped going into hot tubs, believing it might make her symptoms worse. Strangely enough, I also stayed away from hot tubs for years. My stance was: If Debbie can't do it, I don't want to do it either. My stance has changed since then, but guilt is still definitely involved!

Another lesson God has taught me in this is how to care more for others. Debbie used to describe herself as a selfish person, and I can admit I struggle from time to time with selfishness and self-focus. Having someone in my life who is very reliant on others has helped change my perspective on how God wants me to treat others, especially those who are handicapped. I now intentionally look handicapped people in the eye and I look for opportunities to give them assistance. I stay away from using handicapped restrooms. In fact, I never realized the true value of handicapped restrooms until Debbie's need for them grew. Locating one that is truly accessible is a challenge, and then when we discover that someone not handicapped is using it— well, that person just might shrivel under my death stare.

I have discovered I have become extremely protective and defensive of my sister as a handicapped person. My boss once suggested to me that we use the handicapped parking spots in our school parking lot for regular parking, and I responded "Absolutely not!" If Debbie and I are out and about, I expect others to open doors for us. I expect shops to have ramps and easy entry. I expect there to be handrails in bathrooms and even for there to be handicapped port-a-potties. Getting out of the house in general is a challenge for Debbie and other disabled people, and I admire them for taking on that challenge so many times.

Throughout all of this, it has been remarkable to see the providence of God in Debbie's and her family's lives. They have been forced to increase their reliance on God and his ultimate plan, and it has been inspiring for me to watch. I am comforted knowing God has a specific purpose in all this, even though I have yet to figure it out. Thinking of and meditating on heaven and all its glory and perfection truly resonates more with me when I think of heaven being the end to Debbie's physical struggle. This past year I read several books which focused on heaven, and every one of them made me think of what an eternal future holds for Debbie. I know it can be hard to have an eternal perspective on worldly problems, but sometimes that is all I can hold on to.

I do not know what the future holds for Debbie. I pray every day God will heal her, but at the same time I pray that God's will be done in her life. I don't know what God's will is, and it may be that she is never healed while here on earth. Again, I am comforted with a heavenly perspective and know our time on earth is but a drop in the bucket of eternity. Debbie will always be my twin, my sister, and my best friend, and I will do whatever I can to support her. She inspires me daily to find joy, to have self-control, to put others first and to lean on God. She is my hero.

CHAPTER 4

What is Normal?

> "Love so amazing, so divine
> Demands my soul, my life, my all."
>
> –Christopher Norton and Isaac Watts,
> *When I Survey the Wondrous Cross*

What is normal?

How is my new normal different from my old normal?

I don't *like* my new normal. Do I really have to live my life like this?

"God gave us feelings," I have been told over and over. Does this mean it is okay for me to feel negatively about my new normal? Does this mean it's okay to not be able to make up my mind about how I feel?

Because I have often not wanted to be normal, and now I am certainly not.

Because sometimes I want to be treated like everyone else.

Because occasionally I want to be ignored and occasionally I don't.

The definition of normal is typical, usual, expected or conforming to a standard. Whose standard? In a culture of tolerance and easy offense, do I want to conform to this world's current standard? Twenty years ago, one of my favorite praise songs spoke of the desire for the Lord to take my will and conform it to his. The Lord tells us to conform to *his* image. He is not typical, usual, or expected. He is *not* normal.

> " *The Lord tells us to conform to* his *image. He is not typical, usual, or expected. He is* not *normal.*

When I was planning my wedding twenty years ago, I didn't want to do things the way everyone else did. I didn't want the typical or usual wedding. Instead of using bows at pew ends, I used sprigs of boxwood. Instead of a circular layered wedding cake, ours was hexagonal. Instead of attendees throwing rice as we left the reception, well-wishers sprinkled dried flower petals. We purposely folded the service bulletins differently, enjoyed non-traditional music, and used the service to give honor to the Lord.

We tell our children they should not do what everyone else is doing. It's the proverbial "If your friend would jump off a cliff..." Jesus even said to go the narrow road.[1] Why, then, do I want to be treated "normally?" What is the attraction? It's probably because life is harder now. I want my life to go back to the way it was. A part of me wants to pursue normal, and my "old" life could be described that way.

What is normal anyway? One author says it's just a setting on your dryer. But what if my life is never normal again? Are my husband, children, family, and friends ready to experience life this way for as long as I live? Am I?

Besides being in a wheelchair and experiencing several other smaller results of multiple sclerosis, such as an inability to write birthday cards or checks, fortunately I still have the ability to do many things. I am able to converse, electronically pay bills, navigate my phone, and hunt-and-peck on a keyboard. When planning a birthday party for my mother-in-law, I spoke with a caterer on the phone several times before the occasion. When finally meeting in person, I wondered if she was surprised that I was disabled. That I didn't move normally. Should I have let her know I used, at that time, a walker?

When I plan to visit a person who does not know I have a disability, I have gotten into the habit of proactively telling him or her I am in a wheelchair. This seems to be the best option when invited to someone's house or when spending time with relatives I haven't seen for a while. Besides helping all of us feel more comfortable, I need to know details about accessibility and maneuverability. Plus, I have found my health situation resulting in a wheelchair is quite a surprise to those I haven't stayed in contact with; filling them in on the details beforehand helps limit surprise and excess emotion.

Recently I saw an acquaintance I had not seen for roughly six years. She didn't know about my disability and was surprised about it as she asked the reason. She didn't avoid the topic, which I appreciated, and I gave her an abbreviated reply with some tears mixed in. We connected well because she is now experiencing disability through her husband's declining health. As she proudly showed me how a wheelchair lift connected to her vehicle, I realized discussing this resource was indeed welcome and helpful.

It was wonderful to be able to cry with this friend as we commiserated about shared experiences. We cried tears of sadness for the trials we have endured. We cried tears of joy for the lessons we have learned and continue to learn from the Lord. We know we are not living the lives we would choose, but we were able to talk honestly about the balance between walking our paths willingly or walking them grudgingly. We know we can look to each other for support and encouragement during the darkest of days ahead because each of us does indeed understand.

> **“** *We know we are not living the lives we would choose, but we were able to talk honestly about the balance between walking our paths willingly or walking them grudgingly.*

Typically, when in a public setting with others I don't know, I want my disability to be ignored. That way, I don't have to answer questions that might be awkward or cause emotion. However, if a stranger does approach me, it shows their courage and kindness, which I don't easily forget.

Conversely, it is hurtful to be looked over by people with whom I am acquainted. Most people in my small town have seen me without disability aids for years. The use of them causes contemplation and many questions; to openly discuss my story is a welcome relief. It is so awkward being the elephant in the room—a wheelchair cannot be hidden—when the issue is ignored the first time it's seen. I want the opportunity to show transparency about my life even though it has turned out to be unexpected and difficult. Most importantly, I look for the chance to proclaim the Lord's goodness.

When I am the occasional infamous "elephant," the first time being around others who don't address the issue of disability can be uncomfortable. People often do not know what to say nor do they want to say anything offensive, therefore, some don't say anything at all, which I have perceived in the past as being ignored. But being avoided is not the issue; I need to help others feel more comfortable by engaging in conversation with them.

I would like to be talked to like a normal person. I want to be asked about my day, my family, or my activities just like anyone else. A friend recently asked what I was looking forward to in the upcoming season. I appreciated this question greatly because it made me feel normal, and it did not address my disability. Simply talking to friends about things we would normally discuss and never bringing up my health or well-being is refreshing.

Currently, my situation asks a lot of my friends; they show gracious servanthood by picking me up and driving, pushing my wheelchair, and even holding me steady in public bathrooms. Because getting together looks different than it used to, I am thankful for friends who take the time to initiate contact. We have regular coffee dates, filling time by discussing our life happenings and relationships with the Lord. As in the past, it is still my responsibility to reciprocate the friendship. I am genuinely interested in their activities and want to assist however I can—listening to, caring about, and praying for family ventures.

Most of my current friendships existed before I became disabled. I want them to remember me as the person I was. Because I have grown deeply in my faith and trust of the Lord over the last four years, I not only am especially appreciative of friends who have grown in the same way, I hope my deeper faith and trust are evident to them.

> **❝** *Because I have grown deeply in my faith and trust of the Lord over the last four years, I not only am especially appreciative of friends who have grown in the same way, I hope my deeper faith and trust are evident to them.*

One relationship has been rekindled and I have become close to two more women since I've been in a wheelchair. These two new friendships started early in The Decline, when my MS became visible, and I began walking with the assistance of a cane. My cane was not seen as an obstacle, but instead invited transparency, a quality necessary for genuineness. Do I now have a personality that invites new friendships? All these connections are based on some sort of ministry; the Lord is the central figure. Therefore, it is probable the relationships serve a purpose in his kingdom. It is exciting to watch them develop.

Because I am wary of unintentional insensitive remarks, I cherish truly encouraging comments. One of the best comments said during The Decline, in the midst of my new normal, was, "You're still the same Debbie." Unbeknownst to her, my friend said what I needed to hear. Despite undergoing many physical changes and moving in a very different way, my personality remains the same.

"It must be better for God's kingdom that you use a cane than you don't," is another observation I appreciated. Presently, of course, the cane would be upgraded to a wheelchair, but I hope this statement is true. I trust this is how the Lord works in his infinite wisdom—his kingdom should take precedence over my thoughts and feelings of normal.

I hear many more attempts at reassurance, which I genuinely appreciate. When considerate people comfort me by assuring me I will connect well with others who also experience MS, disability, or loss, I know this is true. I have seen proof. My MS diagnosis has propelled me to relate with many and encourage them. My disability is unwanted, but the Lord works in magnificent ways; it has been a great source of connection.

The most frequent comment I hear, said to offer comfort, is regarding how the Lord operates. I am told having MS is not my fault, and the Lord is not punishing me. I have never thought that! I do not imagine the Lord works in that way! But because it is mentioned so often to me, is it that prevalent of a thought? When experiencing difficult times or trials in their lives, do others assume the Lord is punishing them? Yes, the Lord tests us, but he also refines us. He refines us like silver. He wants to make me just like him.

> **"** *Yes, the Lord tests us, but he also refines us. He refines us like silver. He wants to make me just like him.*

Many people have asked me if I experience any pain, and thankfully, I do not. The Lord has kept my foot from slipping as he molds me into his image. "He has preserved our lives and kept our feet from slipping. For you, God, tested us; you refined us like silver. You brought us into prison and laid burdens on our backs...Praise be to God, who has not rejected my prayer or withheld his love from me!" Psalm 66:9-11, 20.

The Lord trains some to be sympathetic, which is having feelings of pity and sorrow for someone else's misfortune, and others to be empathetic, which is having the ability to understand and share the feelings of another. While I do not want to be pitied, I appreciate anyone sharing my disability or feelings. Support groups, a way of empathizing with others by way of truly understanding their situations, as well as meeting other people with MS, have been offered to me on several occasions. It is likely through these channels I would meet others in similar positions. I have not pursued these options yet, but I know for certain it would be therapeutic. Giving and receiving mutual and open support would be welcome. It would almost be a relief to recognize that others are in a similar situation.

I have informally connected with some who also experience the effects of disability in their lives. The sharing of resources, as well as encouraging others with the Lord's purposes and strategies, has been invaluable. From these conversations, I have gained knowledge about mobility aids, travel, and reading material. While befriending a woman whose husband suffered from a similar neurological disease, I have gotten tips on accessible vacation options. Reconnecting with another acquaintance who has a spouse with yet another neurological condition taught me strategies of interacting with others while displaying joy.

Anyone who is visibly different knows to get used to stares, which may stem from either sympathy or pity. Long, interested looks from kids are understandable and make sense; they don't know any better. Volunteering at my children's elementary school definitely invites stares from kids, but it does not bother me. I hope these children are learning that being different is totally acceptable, and a person's demeanor should not be affected by their lack of abilities.

> *Anyone who is visibly different knows to get used to stares*

However, even my nine-year-old daughter notices stares from adults, which are not as easily excusable because adults should know better. These long, interested looks from people who did not know I was disabled are harder to swallow. I experienced this recently while voting. I have learned to steel myself in these public situations and "grin and bear it" when other adults look at me. My preference is for my wheelchair use to be easily discussed. I welcome questions, and I wish they would be asked as I would relish discussing my need for a disability aid. However, these conversations often don't happen; I must be understanding and forgive—necessary components.

I have wondered at times if my wheelchair use is an embarrassment to my children, though I am convinced no matter what I do, what I look like, or how I move, I will be an embarrassment to them at some point in their lives. Every mother is. All three of my children have reassured me that the wheelchair is not embarrassing; in fact, they are used to it. However, being shy in childhood, many things embarrassed me, and I think I would experience this now. Fainting in the heat at high school band camp rates as one of my top embarrassing moments. Religious bumper stickers on my parents' vehicles and admitting my father was a pastor are only some of the other many circumstances that bothered me. Thankfully, these embarrassments were turned around for good! As I matured, I became proud of my parents' public show of faith and the fact that my dad preached the gospel.

After all, if I am clearly embarrassed by being disabled, how do others learn the Lord is good, no matter what? It doesn't matter if I'm at a church event, such as a fall festival, or a very secular event, like my local high school football game, I want the announcement to ring loud and clear that the Lord is indeed good, no matter what. Whether I'm helping with a school fundraiser in a wheelchair or attending graduation receptions in a wheelchair, I desire others to know the Lord is exceedingly, abundantly good. He is good when I'm attending flag football games that have seating amidst uneven ground and a parking area with rough terrain. He is good when using a public restroom that is not handicap accessible and doesn't have any grab bars, much less anything to hold onto.

The Lord is exceedingly, abundantly good even if I am not healed in this lifetime. Even when life looks different than it did for forty-three years. Even though I have lost most of what I was used to. The majority of the previous way I lived. Sometimes I must remind myself of this goodness and look past my current circumstances.

Clinging to Hope

By Debbie's friend Sarah

I've only ever known Debbie since she carried the diagnosis of multiple sclerosis—but when I first met her, I had no idea. We met when a mutual friend introduced us, shortly after my family had moved to the area and didn't know many people. Our children, all similar ages, immediately delighted in each other's company. Of at least equal importance, I right away warmed to Debbie's infectiously positive and fun demeanor. She put me at ease when I awkwardly apologized for bringing extra snacks for my kids who are always hungry, at least for snack foods. My unsightly pauses were easily filled by her with sincere questions about my family, my interests, and my history. I remember little bits of my protective armor chipping away as we freely talked about favorite books and movies, and as we shared knowing smiles while our children played with unabashed silliness, any pretenses long since abandoned.

She told me she had grown up as the daughter of a Lutheran pastor, and for a Lutheran pastor's wife, who had just moved to a primarily Mennonite area, it was comforting and refreshing to meet someone who understood. I didn't have to explain that part; she got it. And she also understood that the role of the pastor's wife, while an important piece of me, is not my defining trait. I, too, am just another girl with hang-ups and struggles who daily relearns that Jesus' grace and mercy are all I truly need.

Debbie has continued, through the short six years I have known her, to demonstrate grace and transparency with me. We've shared hard family struggles that I didn't feel comfortable telling anyone else. She continues to reveal to me a beauty and graceful strength as her weakness has increased. Even in her wheelchair, she seeks not her own pity or attention, but rather keeps her eyes focused outward, ever loving her neighbor well.

These past few years, I have witnessed Debbie becoming more disabled and more reliant upon her wheelchair. While I have experience helping patients with disabilities in my work, Debbie is the closest person to me I have seen go through this process. Grief for Debbie and for her family has knocked upon my heart and mind repeatedly. Where disability was often an objective diagnosis or stage before, it has now presented itself as a physical presence that forces Debbie to rely on help from her husband, children, and friends. While I have grieved with her and quietly noticed her deteriorating physical strength, I have been struck even more by her pervasive hope and persistence.

One of my favorite verses in the Bible is, "In the world you will have tribulation. But take heart; I have overcome the world."[1] Why do terrible things happen in this world? Why do people get sick? Why did Debbie get MS? There is so much I don't understand. And there are many things that feel unfair. Many times, God does not reveal to us what he is doing and why he allows some things to happen. But I do know that he loves us. He loves Debbie, and he sees her, and he knows her. And I know Debbie clings to his promises. And he is with Debbie always, "to the end of the age."[2]

Three sisters sitting at a lake before Luella's MS diagnosis. From left, Celeste Eggers MacMillan, Luella Eggers Krause, Ruth Eggers Kalow. Minnesota, 1940.

Grandmother Luella Eggers Krause, as a newlywed, before MS diagnosis. Minnesota, 1943.

The Krause family on vacation in Texas.
From left, Tim, Mom, Beth, me, Matt, Dad. Texas, 1986.

High school graduation with my twin. From left, Mom,
me, Dad, Beth. Kansas, 1992.

Phil and me the year of MS diagnosis. Colorado, 1999.

Photo/Janet Post

Our wedding day. Kansas, 2001.

My first half marathon with friend Carisa Funk.
Kansas, 2004.

Carisa and me at our last Vintage Soiree pop-up sale.
Kansas, 2016.

Family photo shoot with my babies. Kansas, 2014.

Twins! Kansas, 2016.

Mother-daughter kayaking. Oklahoma, 2019.

Enjoying my three-wheeled recumbent bike. Kansas, 2019.

A dip in the Mediterranean Sea. Maritima,
Mediterranean Sea, Israel, 2020.

Where young shepherd David slew the giant Goliath.
Valley of Elah, Israel, 2020.

Staycation! Kansas, 2020.

Miniature golf during staycation. Kansas, 2020.

Married twenty years. Kansas, 2020.

Newest family photo shoot. Kansas, 2021.

Hiking the Reservoir. Kansas, 2021.

Exploring a nature trail. Kansas, 2021.

CHAPTER 5

Loss Upon Loss Upon Loss

"I have held many things in my hands, and I have lost them all; but whatever I have placed in God's hands, that I still possess."

–Martin Luther

Loss. The death of a loved one. Separated from a child in a store. Misplacing keys or a wallet. Even lost in the woods.

Loss is difficult. Sometimes it is permanent, sometimes it is temporary. The loss I experience is neither of these. It is ongoing.

Though I have minimal experience with the death of a loved one, I am well acquainted with the cost of secondary-progressive multiple sclerosis. The price seems to be life as I knew it; expenses have been mobility, hobbies, a job, and a master bedroom. However, my marriage and my three amazing children have escaped danger.

I have dealt with my losses in many ways, such as crying, praying, questioning, and talking openly with others. As I mourn through various expressions, I've learned understanding and nonjudgment are necessary when responding to others' grief and the ways in which they mourn. Grief can be demonstrated in many forms, and there is not a prescribed way to do so. I have appreciated the flexibility and acceptance others have had for my sadness.

Naturally, I spent several months grieving for the loss of the life I once knew. I still grieve these casualties and to count them would be impossible. To consider them would be overwhelming. New losses happen almost daily—I have had to alter, discontinue, or decrease almost all my previous activities. Therefore, I want to do whatever I am still able, whether it is because of sheer determination, persistence, or independence. I don't want to lose the ability to do anything else. The adage seems to be true, "If you don't use it, you'll lose it."

> **"** *I spent several months grieving for the loss of the life I once knew. I still grieve these casualties and to count them would be impossible. To consider them would be overwhelming.*

To ponder these losses would be painful, so I purposely choose not to. Some psychologists might say this is either denial or stuffing my feelings, but I consider it good mental health and self-preservation. I will deal with these losses in the best way possible for me; perhaps the Lord has equipped me with determination and optimism for this very reason.

Because the casualties I have experienced are major and ongoing, there seems to be no end to my grief or loss. However, as long as I unshakably follow Jesus, it is important for me to grieve well. Being an extremely emotional person, this does lend to crying often. Sometimes I certainly like to talk about my losses, though I do not always verbalize them because of my tendency to cry. Crying in front of others can be embarrassing and uncomfortable, especially as it occurs repeatedly in front of family, friends, household help, or strangers. I do not want others to become impatient with my constant crying or my eyes watering. I want others to know I believe, without a doubt, the Lord is good. Crying might seem to betray this deeply held belief. But the Lord has a purpose for everything, and so I often wonder about the purpose of my tears.

> **"** *I believe, without a doubt, the Lord is good.*

My frequent tears also occasionally demonstrate I react with fear when forgetting the Lord's promises to always be with me. I have often thought I cannot handle disability any longer, and it is frequently said the Lord will not give us more than we can bear. But the Lord does not say those words. First Corinthians 10:13 says the Lord will "not let you be *tempted* beyond what you can bear" (emphasis mine). The Lord might give us unbearable times because he wants to see how we handle it, particularly if we remember to sustain ourselves only with him and his word.

In this verse, the *New Living Translation* uses the words "be able to stand up under it." A few years ago, when he was nine, Thomas entered a calm wave pool. When the waves began, he could no longer swim or stand up under the weight of the water. Not using a mobility aid yet, I jumped in and quickly swam to him in order to hold him up above the surface. This potentially overwhelming situation resolved quickly, and this incident brought to life the suitable phrase, "My lifeguard walks on water."[1] We almost needed additional physical assistance from a nearby guard, but the Lord stood us up through this sudden difficulty.

Joni Eareckson Tada reminds us a day is coming when sin is forever and completely obliterated. She encourages us to find peace in this defeat of our enemy and reminds us of Romans 16:20, "The Lord of peace will soon crush Satan under your feet." Satan is said to be a snake or like a snake. If I ever have the misfortune of being bit by a poisonous snake, I hope anti-venom would be nearby. Anti-venom consisting of lamb blood is found to be the most effective. The enemy is being defeated by the blood of the lamb, as described in Revelation 12:11.

> " *The enemy is being defeated by the blood of the lamb.*

King David said to the Lord in Psalm 16:11, "you will fill me with joy in your presence." Written over five hundred years after this, Nehemiah 8:10 says "The joy of the LORD is your strength." Following this logic, if I get joy from being in the Lord's presence, then I should be full of strength. But because I unarguably am not strong physically, this must refer to emotional, spiritual, or mental strength.

Sometimes I question my emotional strength because I seem to cry often. It would be a mistake to assume a show of emotion means a lack of strength. My spiritual strength has come from being pulled close to the Lord during these continual losses, and my mental strength has risen out of enduring loss. I can still face life with contentment and peace.

The Lord is said to "keep track of all my sorrows."[2] He has collected all my tears in a bottle. He records each one in his book. Just how big is this bottle? Does he have an enormous cistern for me? Is it mine only? Because I could most likely fill it by myself. And how about the book where he records my tears? Does it have lots of pages? Are they tear-stained?

Does the Lord cry with me? Does he grieve with me over my losses? The Lord never says that he cries with us, but, according to his compassionate character, I completely and faithfully believe he does. After all, he shed tears over the entire city of Jerusalem lamenting its demise[3] and he wept over the death of a friend.[4] As I have shed many tears over the past four years, it brings great comfort picturing the Lord crying with me.

Also comforting are the words of the Lord in Isaiah, "In the same way I will not cause pain without allowing something new to be born."[5] Our all-knowing sovereign Lord is acutely aware of my situation, he recognizes it is quite painful, and he will even allow something new to come from it. Sorrow is not meaningless!

" Sorrow is not meaningless!

I did eventually find meaning through the painful and long international adoption process. When I met other adoptive parents who had also waited more than six years for their daughter from China, I felt relief. I was glad to know other families' wait was the same length as ours. Unfortunately, I did not meet these families until the process was basically over, as this was before the days of frequent posting on social media. Mutual encouragement could have made the adoption process easier and the waiting time more bearable. As difficult as it was, it was obvious the long wait was a tool of the Lord to strengthen and make my marriage relationship rock-solid.

Are trials in my past preparation for the current losses? These troubles resulted in noticeable spiritual growth. Without a doubt, infertility was the most difficult to bear and therefore instigated a deeper intimacy with the Lord. Six years filled with fertility clinics, negative pregnancy tests, and failed domestic adoption attempts culminated in entering the world of international adoption. Being witness to the Lord's love and provision for me during those years is irreplaceable, and this time shaped who I am today as a wife, mother, friend, daughter, and sister.

But the timing and provision in my life cannot be compared to another's. Though my current series of losses is considerably tougher than my struggles with infertility inasmuch as becoming disabled has been more demanding, this does not mean the struggles—fertility or otherwise—are not difficult.

Please join me in agreeing to never act as if you understand a situation that is foreign to you.

Please join me in not categorizing the affairs of others.

Please realize you simply need to listen, stay quiet, and pray.

I know it is tempting to offer condolences or encouragement by repeating Scripture or repeating an overused cliché, but it's probably been heard before by the hurting. I cannot emphasize it enough—your job is to listen, stay quiet, and pray.

As much as my fertility issues seem minor in comparison to this present chain of events, being disabled has taught me to similarly chase after the Lord and to cling to him in trials. These lessons are continuous and won't be finished until I am in heaven. With the goals of contentment and joy, and a decreased concern of the world's views, I need strength from the Lord daily. The insights into the Lord's workings and reliance upon his strength, gained from the heartache of infertility, have far-reaching effects that will last the rest of my life.

> *The insights into the Lord's workings and reliance upon his strength, gained from the heartache of infertility, have far-reaching effects that will last the rest of my life.*

Some of my losses involve work for the Lord, and it is puzzling the Lord would take these opportunities away. Being a tool of the Lord to make an impact on others' lives has been important to me and worthwhile. No longer able to move around at an average pace or travel easily decreases my ability to connect with and minister to others. I had been teaching a fifth-grade girls' Sunday School class. This good thing, this work for the Lord, has been forced to end because of my mobility difficulties.

Other losses involve previous interests or activities of mine. For example, typing has always been something I loved, and I have vivid memories of being eleven years old and sitting, without being prompted, in an upstairs home office practicing typing on an electric typewriter. Later, to help supplement our income while staying home, I worked as a medical transcriptionist. Transcription income is based on speed and accuracy of typing, therefore, when my hand and finger muscles slowed during The Decline, my typing productivity became visibly worse. Resigning from this ten-year profession became the only option, and I did so with feelings of great loss.

Being able to drive and transport oneself anywhere is an overlooked freedom that is often taken for granted. My ability to handle a vehicle is different now, and occasionally I wonder if and when it will be necessary to surrender the privilege of operating my van. Currently, I limit myself to only driving in town or to nearby small towns. Because I was previously a very independent person, this feels extremely constrictive as I have lost the spontaneity of going anywhere I want during the school day. Seeing the pressure this puts on my husband to run errands for me, including transporting the kids to their various activities, is challenging. Though he does not mind being the primary chauffeur—he does teach driver's education after all—it is still trying for me. My self-sufficiency is decreasing. Driving my van is a show of freedom, as were kayaking and riding with my three-wheeled recumbent bicycle. Though truly enjoying still water around my kayak, it became too challenging to balance and row; this loved hobby has ended. However, though I am reluctant to admit it, my electric wheelchair is also a source of independence. Though the sitting may go on forever and without end, I like having the ability to maneuver it myself.

Serving my family in the kitchen is another difficult loss. Though my husband is naturally service-minded and does not mind the additional duties of cooking and washing dishes, I am bothered I can't help. I have given up the dishwasher, sink, cabinets, and refrigerator. Kitchen paraphernalia is arranged and cleaned differently. Upkeep of the rest of the house, as well as the way in which it is done, is usually determined by others' standards. Not being the primary person in control of all that happens in my kitchen and other rooms of my home is certainly a challenge, but because the Lord has taught me invaluable lessons through other difficulties, I realize this undoubtedly could be yet another exercise to teach me about control.

Outdoor work was a previous love of mine. Whether it was digging, cutting, landscaping, clearing out, or transplanting, I had a fondness for putting on my gardening gloves and getting them dirty. Flower beds need to be watered, weeded, or raked, and I have been reluctant to give up working outside in them. Currently, when the season calls for perennials to be cut down or divided, I rely on someone else to do these things. While I cannot be as physically involved as I would like, I still try to manage their care by asking for others' assistance.

Discontinued use of my basement office is perhaps one of the most difficult casualties—stairs are too laborious to climb to make its use worthwhile. My office space was generally untouched by anyone else in my family, and I held dear its privacy. For eight years, I spent night hours in that small room typing medical transcriptions. More importantly, time was devoted to deepening my relationship with the Lord. The precious moments in that sacred space remain as dear memories, and though the location of this time devoted to the Lord has changed, I have learned the physical location of my "quiet time" does not matter to Him. He is more concerned about the position of the heart. Despite having an empty house during the school day, a home still has potential to hold several distractions. I must forego picking up throw pillows and blankets from the floor, as well as loading the dishwasher, in order to have discipline to spend time with the Lord.

> " *The precious moments with the Lord in that sacred space remain as dear memories.*

Many other things I used to be interested in or take pride in are now a loss, such as my running ability, piano playing, project completion, typing speed, antique business, house cleanliness, decorating love, and efficiency in all things. Most of the time, I do not care about these things anymore. Paul states, "I once thought these things were valuable, but now I consider them worthless because of what Christ has done."[8] I try not to be interested in my achievements anymore, and to instead treat them as if they are worthless.

As my children get older, attention turns to their achievements. For example, Thomas recently shot a deer with a crossbow.

Normally our whole family would accompany him to retrieve the animal, but I was not able to go because of the amount of walking on bumpy ground. My wheelchair could not navigate the adventure. I patiently waited at home during the search, realizing I needed to take advantage of the time I had alone. Staying home is becoming commonplace—as a busy mom, it is a benefit I am learning to appreciate more and more.

An additional activity I have had to forego in many ways is placing Christmas decorations around the house. Decorating for the holiday is important to my family and me, but I am only interested in doing this with a fraction of the enthusiasm displayed in the past. Attempting to put decorations in place from a wheelchair while not being able to stand or reach very far is a challenge. I can no longer put many ornaments on our live Christmas tree in the living room or stand on a chair to place them near the top. Fortunately, Thomas, Matthias, and Laura are old enough to do this without breaking very many, and Phil is tall enough to place them at the top. My kids may hastily hang up the outside décor, but I am no longer concerned about its arrangement. Since they can do what I cannot, I am grateful for their efforts, and their willingness to brave the cold with arms full of garland and Christmas lights is more important than perfect placement.

My children's eagerness to hug me is equally important and meaningful. As awkward as it is, my family has gotten used to hugging me while I am sitting, as have friends. I need this display of affection. It makes me feel happy, and hugs have the potential to improve any mood, as does music. Singing, whether impromptu or along with songs on the radio or in church, is another casualty. I no longer have the lung capacity or muscle strength to carry a tune—my ability to sing on pitch, to sing with volume, or to sing clearly is affected. Though my family jokingly does not miss my vocals, I certainly miss the capability to break out in song.

Physical differences aren't the only changes I'm experiencing. I have recognized changes in my memory, speed of recall, word use, and decision-making. While statistics vary, researchers tend to agree that about 65 percent of people with MS have some type of cognitive impairment. Along with others who have multiple sclerosis, I don't know if my cognitive changes are associated with MS or simply normal aging. This makes deciphering details regarding health insurance, Medicare, and other long-term planning difficult; however, I now have a brilliant excuse for hare-brained moments or erratic actions!

I no longer spend time scrolling through social media to look at the pictures friends have posted. Though I know the photos are a beautiful representation of their lives, my own posts will probably never have pictures of me standing in them. It would be dishonest to portray my life as if it wasn't extremely difficult to bear. Yet, my social media followers need to know the Lord will sustain me through his word, the Bible. "These words hold me up in bad times; yes, your promises rejuvenate me."[9] I need a gulp of fresh air in the midst of my loss. Inhaling and exhaling the Lord rejuvenates my soul. I am not made whole physically, but I am becoming a spiritual restoration in the midst of my trials. I will walk with my head held high![10]

> " *It would be dishonest to portray my life*
> *as if it wasn't extremely difficult to bear.*

Though known throughout the world as actors, some may not know that Christina Applegate, Montel Williams, and Teri Garr have been diagnosed with multiple sclerosis. It gives me a sense of camaraderie to know others struggle with the same disease. In this stage of my MS, as I now read *Momentum*, I realize besides the difficult-to-read stories, it does contain helpful resources and information. Looking past stories of challenging situations helps me focus on what is most helpful—connectedness. I feel a great tie with the MS community.

> *I want to encourage others to be real by being transparent myself.*

Occasionally I am asked to talk with those who are either facing a diagnosis of multiple sclerosis or currently have the diagnosis, and I enjoy these interactions, partly because they provide connectedness. I try to be optimistic during the conversations, but now that I use a wheelchair, I fear others may be discouraged by the sight of it. I do not want them to be wary, either, of sharing their own struggles because I now use a wheelchair. My disease has worsened in progression, but I do not want this challenge to make another feel as if their own disease struggle should not be addressed. My physical being may not be promising, but it does not mean my spiritual being cannot build hope in others. I want to genuinely express empathy, show concern, and share comfort with those who are hurting from ailments. I want to encourage others to be real by being transparent myself.

Putting full hope and trust in the Lord is not easy while becoming disabled or experiencing any trial. Off and on, I have experienced plenty of fear during The Decline, especially when it began. I kept asking the Lord to halt my diminishing abilities, but the answer was continually "no." My disabilities have always gotten worse. Amazingly, the future is not as scary as it used to be. To ward off this despair, I purposefully do not think about attending my children's graduations or weddings in a wheelchair because to be afraid of what is to come would be to defy the Lord. He tells me over 350 times in the Bible to not be afraid.

Since I have not been healed, it could be assumed the Lord is not answering my prayer. Others' disappointment, as well as my own, of continued disability after prayer is noticeable. I still need assistance walking, and my diagnosis of multiple sclerosis remains. However, the Lord always answers prayer, just not consistently in the way I might want. He responds to requests, but sometimes the answers are "no" or "not yet." Though others may conclude from my present situation the Lord is not listening, nor does he care, I am confident of the opposite: "For the eyes of the Lord are on the righteous and his ears are attentive to their prayer."[11]

Jesus' words from the Sermon on the Mount bring relief to any concerns:

> "You're blessed when you're at the end of your rope. With less of you, there is more of God and his rule.

"You're blessed when you feel you've lost what is most dear to you. Only then can you be embraced by the One most dear to you.

"You're blessed when you're content with just who you are— no more, no less. That's the moment you find yourselves proud owners of everything that can't be bought."[12]

Though the Lord's "no" is excruciatingly demanding, life goes on and I must face it daily.

Asking the Hard Questions

By Debbie's friend Lynette

Debbie and I became instant friends when our husbands, who teach together, introduced us. We spent many hours walking or jogging, sitting in each other's living rooms baring our souls, raising our two-days-apart-sons, and sharpening one another in our individual faith journeys. I had always known Debbie had MS, but it had never impeded the life I'd known her to live. Her symptoms and disease were in remission from the time I met her until more than ten years into our friendship. In those ten-plus years, I had to work hard to keep up with Debbie, both as we exercised and did life. She was always seemingly "running circles" around me.

All of this changed, rather abruptly, as Debbie's MS began to progress. To be honest, I distanced myself for a bit, as I tried to process what my role was in these changes. I didn't want our friendship to change, but it had to, both in good ways and hard ways. Any life change, including each of the children we added to our families, changed our friendship. This just seemed a bit different.

The questions that ran through my head were:

"Does she have anyone who is asking the hard questions such as 'How are you really doing, beyond the surface? How has this been hard for you? Where do you see God in all of this? Are you able to grieve what has been lost?'"

"Does she want anyone to ask those questions, or are those for her to process with God and Phil?"

"What can I do to best help and yet allow Debbie to feel most 'normal?'"

My fears of asking the wrong thing at the wrong time or giving unsolicited ideas or advice caused me to continue to keep my distance, until the Lord impressed on my heart that he has given me the Holy Spirit to guide and direct my words and actions. It was then I surrendered my feeble efforts to be the friend Debbie needed/wanted and allowed the Holy Spirit to direct our friendship. I prayed often for guidance as to what would encourage and strengthen Debbie most in the times we were together.

Regarding disability, my perspective only goes as far as watching family members and how they have handled sudden disabilities. I can't personally understand how it feels for life to change so quickly and be out of my control. However, I have an aunt who has battled a disability that took away her ability to walk, in a matter of days. Her perspective has made an impact on me, just as Debbie's has. When I asked my aunt how she handles all she's been through, she responded she sees two choices in front of her: to sit and be depressed about what she's lost or to find joy in the journey and see the good in it. I feel Debbie has done this in many ways. Watching them battle for joy and hope in the midst of the hard has shown me that while disability has limited their movements and activities, it has not stolen their ability to move, sense, or be active. It just looks different than it used to. So now Debbie and I don't walk or jog together, but we watch our sons play sports together. We go to lunch instead of making lunch together. We serve on committees together instead of going shopping (our husbands should thank us). My friend has different abilities because of her disability, but she is the same wonderful friend, just much wiser and stronger for what she has journeyed through. Her abilities to spend time with the Lord, interceding for others, and writing this book are among some of the ones I admire the most.

Debbie's heart for Jesus and the desire for her and her family to continue to love and serve the people around them, have been so encouraging to watch. As we've prayed in faith for healing, I struggle with how little I know my big God and his ways. There have been times when I've cried out in frustration:

"Lord, we've believed with faith as small as a mustard seed that this mountain would be moved from Debbie's life, why has it not been moved?[1] We know and believe you are a God who still does miracles. When Jesus went among those who were sick, he healed *every* one of them who came to him. Why not Debbie? She is your servant, she has children to raise and people to disciple. Why is she not being healed?"

When Jesus healed the blind man in the Gospel of John, the people asked who had sinned, the man or his parents, that he would have been born blind. "Neither this man nor his parents sinned," said Jesus, 'but this happened so that the works of God might be displayed in him.'"[2]

While I don't understand all of God's mysterious ways or the plan he has for Debbie in her journey with multiple sclerosis, I do know that Debbie's love for Jesus and trust in him have allowed God's mighty works to be displayed. I am thankful to have a small part in this story God is weaving together for good.

CHAPTER 6

> "We pray for the big things and forget to give thanks for the ordinary, small (and yet really not small) gifts."
>
> –Dietrich Bonhoeffer, *Life Together: The Classic Exploration of Christian Community*

How regularly do I talk about my illness? How often do I voice that it affects everything I do and, likely, even how I think? How often do I ask for help? What if I don't need the help that's offered?

Communicating with those closest to me can be difficult anyway, but regarding my disease, it is even harder now. Letting them know my needs, as well as what I am able or unable to do, is challenging because of my independence and uncomplaining personality. Those closest to me—my husband and my children—have witnessed The Decline every day. Other close family and friends have witnessed most of it but have not experienced the gritty details.

The first sixteen years of marriage to Phil were not challenged by disability; Phil was not daunted by the diagnosis of multiple sclerosis as he proposed. The disease and potential of disability were some of the furthest things from our minds. For more than fifteen years, we enjoyed many outdoor adventures: honeymooning in Alaska, snow skiing in Colorado, water skiing in Iowa, tubing in Missouri, a mission trip in Haiti, an adoption in China, touring in Israel, hiking in the Ozarks, kayaking and boating with our kids, and becoming nauseated at amusement parks. Even a trip to Malawi, Africa, that was planned early in The Decline was excitedly anticipated, but it was thwarted by the worldwide pandemic. We have enjoyed roaming junk and antique shops together, leading us to dream about designing and creating our own décor and furniture when our children have moved on to future endeavors. We're looking forward to doing what any empty nesters might dream of doing in the future. Maybe we'll enjoy outdoor time together, picking up the hobby of hunting once again. Phil introduced me to this sport before we had children and I had mild success. I enjoyed hiking through nature with my husband; obviously it will be done in a very different way now, but I look forward to again tracking animals in the great outdoors.

When The Decline started, we had no inclination how, when, or if it would end. Having a husband who is very serious about his faith has made a huge difference. I am fully aware that life would be even harder without such a supportive and helpful spouse. Those with chronic diseases are less likely to marry, and if they are married, they are more likely to divorce than a nondisabled couple. The divorce rate of couples who have one spouse with a disability is rising. Disability within a marriage causes stress—the stress of caring for a disabled spouse, and the stress of coping with limited finances. Surveys even suggest the rate of divorce is higher among those with multiple sclerosis than other conditions. This data is not encouraging at all. But the Lord has more influence over my views than the world does, and I know that he is unconcerned about the latest statistic.

> " *When The Decline started, we had no inclination how, when, or if it would end.*

I recognize I am married to a man who takes his wedding vows and covenant very seriously. I do as well, and I do not want the possibility of my disability affecting the success of our marriage. The idea that disability may affect us for the rest of our lives is disappointing, overwhelming, and disheartening. Enriching our marriage is a top priority. Potentially scary data brings up many questions that need to be considered regarding the current status of our lives.

How often do I talk about my illness and the specifics of my struggle? Do I tell him about every time I fall? Do I mention every new symptom? When do I ask for help? How should I handle every loss?

What about future costs and planning? How does this affect our finances? Do we need to start saving for long-term care?

During family times, how do I truthfully portray peace and joy? During days home alone, how do I best spend my time? During mealtimes, how do I give up my kitchen and the preparation of food for my family?

Though our life together is at an all-time high level of difficulty, there is no one I would rather have on my side, besides the Lord, than Phil. He knows me best and all the ins and outs of my disability and mobility. He is my biggest advocate and my strongest ally. He has quietly listened to my repeated shedding of tears. He has held a trash can when I experienced the first side effects of a new medication. For the last four years, he has physically stabilized me by always being ready to offer a hand or arm when I move unsteadily.

Though marriage is not easy, and on some days when conflict, tears, and hurt feelings seem to be commonplace, they become far outweighed by laughter, forgiveness, and smiles. Jokes frequently fly around the room as Phil's comedy is well-timed and often needed. As he can be very goofy and funny, Phil's quick, silly sarcasm and antics are a delight to his kids, his students, and me. It is a talent passed to the next generation— Thomas has a knack for stand-up comedy, and sometimes keeps me in stitches.

But occasionally I wish Phil and I had known and recognized our lasts: our last walk together, our last time getting in or out of a vehicle unencumbered by a walking aid, or our last time eating out without making sure my wheelchair could fit under the table. I wish I would have known it was the last time we traveled overnight without taking along a shower chair, or the last time we planted our vegetable garden together.

" Occasionally I wish Phil and I had known and recognized our lasts.

When we first met on a blind date, February 21, 1996, we would not have predicted disability would be on the forefront of our lives over twenty-one years later.

When we were engaged on March 1, 2001, we would not realize our love for each other would be tested by the raging furnace of disability.

When we were married on July 28, 2001, we didn't know we were making a covenant to each other and the Lord that would eventually become complicated and demanding to live out several years in the future.

When we celebrated Phil's fortieth birthday next to the Green Monster at Fenway Park, we didn't realize that in less than ten years, we would no longer be able to easily navigate a public transportation system.

Nevertheless, I would do it all over again.

Our children, for the most part, do not remember times in the past when their mom was not disabled, though looking at photos of earlier years does help jog their memories. The advantage of forgetting my abilities is they don't have as much of a sense of loss as I do because this is, and always has been, life for them. Life with a disabled mother cannot be compared to life without one because they don't know or remember otherwise. In their memories, a comparison can't even be made. My Aunt Jean feels similarly about growing up with her mother. "In spite of the challenges, I would not trade my childhood years for anything," Jean said. "Truly, I feel blessed that Mother and her MS are a significant part of my life story."

> " *Our children, for the most part, do not remember times in the past when their mom was not disabled.*

However, my MS is a challenging topic to broach with my children. Perhaps we should have talked about my disability more and in more detail during The Decline. Maybe we should have explained it more. Maybe we should have talked more about what was going on. We didn't know much ourselves, of course, and were barely holding our own heads above water. We suddenly had to navigate a completely new way of doing life. Maybe we should have explained my body's physical decline better to our kids. We'll never know exactly the correct direction to proceed in this blurry gray matter.

"Is Mom handicapped?" asked my oldest son when in an airport, as we went ahead through shorter lines reserved for the disabled. While being handicapped was a tough realization that Phil and I had come to, we had never talked about that word with the kids. We never told our kids that now I fit a label. We never explained to them that our family is now visibly different because of my disability. We never told them this major change in our lives made us live differently because of our trust in the Lord. Because there is no cure for MS and no known cause, unfortunately I cannot reassure my children that they will never have it. At this point, experts suggest the lone possible benefit of vitamin D, taken for the purpose of aiding prevention.

Recently a first cousin of mine—my Aunt Karen's daughter—was diagnosed with multiple sclerosis. The genetics of my family would be an interesting study, and now there is even more reason to wish for a cure.

Matthias is particularly athletic and enjoys playing any sort of sport either indoors or outdoors. Because I enjoyed playing with him when he was younger, he was used to me being outside, actively joining him in a game. As this became more and more difficult and then eventually impossible for me, when Matthias was the young age of seven, he had a challenging time understanding my disability. At that time early in The Decline, he could remember when I used to be able to do outdoor games with him. He was confused as to why I could not anymore. Perhaps this was a time Phil and I should have talked with him specifically about the progression of my disease. Nonetheless, as he grew older, he unquestionably comprehended the circumstances, and he now plays "porch bocce ball" with the family and kindly tries to think of creative ways I can play with him. Though not athletically strenuous for anyone else in the family, porch bocce ball was adapted to my need to throw a heavy ball while holding onto a railing of the porch. As we all try to toss our balls as close to the smaller marker ball as possible, I relish the camaraderie, competition, and smack talk. Making it even more meaningful is the discovery that bocce developed from a game played in the early Roman Empire and now is a hotly contested sport in the Paralympics.

Of all my kids, Matthias has the best memory, so it is not a surprise he can remember a time when his mom could actively play with him outdoors. He also can remember a few occasions when I walked with him into school. I would love to have the chance to do so again. I would love to kneel next to his desk during holiday parties at school to make Christmas or Valentine crafts. I miss gluing yarn and spreading glitter while next to his school desk. I miss joining other moms in passing out sugary treats and sweetened juice drinks. On the other hand, Matthias is also the child who remembers it being a challenge to help me maneuver on stairs, get into a vehicle, and move around in general. Only some memories are worth recalling.

> **"** *I would love to have the chance to do so again.*

These days, I get to our vehicles by riding my motorized wheelchair down a ramp my husband built in the garage. I then motor to the door of the vehicle and transfer into its seat. My kids argue about whose turn it is to take the wheelchair away from the vehicle or "call dibs" on it. As the son of a mother who used a wheelchair, my father has similar memories. "I was pleased to push Mom's wheelchair whenever I could," he said.

I am so glad the kids find fun in my disability. When the enjoyment wears off, my hope is they don't mind continuing to move my wheelchair—I will still need to trade positions. I know it is an extra step for them to move wheelchairs around, especially when their dad is not present. When we arrive at our destination, they need to get my lighter, foldable wheelchair out of the back of the van, not to mention return it there. They even have to wheel the smaller chair to meet me at the driver's door and make sure I get in safely. They are all wonderful at doing this and they ensure it is done carefully. Occasionally they ask me to stay in the van when they run brief errands, such as getting books from the library. This is absolutely acceptable because it is definitely more effort for me to go into a public building. When they ask for a break, I unquestionably give it. I will not take advantage of their graciousness, and I will not impose upon their kindness.

Being a mom is wonderful and difficult at the same time. As a mother who has made many parenting mistakes and has several parenting regrets, I have prayed my children experience amnesia regarding times I, too, would like to forget. One of these instances happened roughly a year and a half ago. On a summer mid-afternoon when our whole family was running errands and my husband wanted to spend more time in a store, the rest of us went out to the vehicle to wait. We happened to be using our truck with a high step-up entrance. My body gets more fatigued in the afternoons, and it happened to be my body's weakest time of the day when we returned to the truck. It took several efforts to get me into the passenger seat. My kids were determined in their efforts, and eventually we had success. Most likely, after we collected ourselves, this was a time I should have discussed my declining mobility with the kids. To encourage them, I should have told them my body typically experiences weakness in the mid-afternoon.

Being a mom is wonderful and difficult at the same time.

Since then, my sons have expressed their dislike for helping me when I fall or need to take a step up. Both of them are now physically capable of giving aid and each are servant-minded; therefore, the aversion must stem from an emotional cost. This is excruciating for me to know. All three, Thomas, Matthias, and Laura, are impressively quick to stop their own activities and give help when I need it, but I am afraid it will take away from them pursuing their own interests. Despite efforts to normalize our life, my disability is harder on them than I had hoped. Living with a mother who is disabled can affect the ability to go places and the activities we do. My hope is that my children never feel they have already or will, in the future, miss out on something because of my disability, or that they will feel something was stolen from their lives. My life experiences testify we grow in difficult circumstances, but this is not what I would have chosen for them. "How long must I struggle with anguish in my soul, with sorrow in my heart every day?"[1] asks King David in Psalm 13, speaking pain and lament, but he ends the psalm with, "But I trust in your unfailing love. I will rejoice because you have rescued me."[2] Trust is a repeated theme in the Psalms and is a repeated theme for me as well, as my family walks this road.

Trust is a repeated theme in the Psalms and is a repeated theme for me as well, as my family walks this road.

Aunt Karen's estimation is, through Luella's MS her siblings and she learned to trust solely in the Lord, and the Lord's love and care would never fail them. My hope is my children are learning the same lesson. Laura has said she has learned the Lord is always caring through tough times. Matthias chimes in by saying he is glad the Lord is with him when times are hard, especially as he is now more aware of my movements than in the past, particularly if I am about to slip and fall. Though watching me falter is difficult for him, helping prevent a fall is worth having to observe my movements. Laura agrees and admits paying attention to my movements in order to prevent a fall is wearing.

All three of my children have become extremely helpful and empathetic young people. They know to open doors for others, as well as move objects on the floor if needed. Thomas even said he thinks he is a better worker because of my disability, which is a trait I wish would have developed in him through different circumstances.

My father credits his mother's disability for his own advocacy for those with disabilities, a sensitivity to those who are disabled, and his tender heart to families with one who is disabled. He believes it is best to treat people with handicaps like everyone else, particularly by greeting them and not ignoring them. As I try to teach these qualities to my children, getting to this point has seemed overwhelming and occasionally unobtainable. I am very thankful they are service-minded, but this quality often doesn't come naturally and instead needs instruction. As my husband Phil loves to help others, they are beginning to copy his actions. Recently during a spring break trip, when shopping and visiting a site with minimal accommodations for those with mobility handicaps, each of my three children expressed thoughts about their futures—they would make accessibility easier when able, such as inclusive design of two-story buildings, sidewalks, and parking options. Laura even expressed this thought at two different times during the short vacation. Gratitude for their compassionate thoughts swept over me.

An unspoken prayer of mine is that my children will not be embarrassed their mother is in a wheelchair. Though all three of them say it is not so now, I hope this can always be said. To my relief, Thomas recently stated, "When you live with a disabled person, you get used to it. It's not different; you just get used to it." My father repeats these thoughts when remembering growing up with his mother in a wheelchair, "I never felt any embarrassment…Nothing seemed hard about it. It was just how life was for us."

> **"** *An unspoken prayer of mine is that my children will not be embarrassed their mother is in a wheelchair.*

Aunt Jean says, "When I see someone in a wheelchair, I wonder the reason. I tend to observe people with physical limitations in places like airports to watch if they need assistance. I do think I am more attentive to individuals who might need an extra hand or even conversation."

One wintry morning after church, then six-year-old Laura asked, "Why do we always need to be careful with Mom on the ice?" As I considered this, I realized my daughter sees me as not having a handicap. Hallelujah! What more does my heart yearn for, than my kids to not see my disability?

The Decline has drastically affected my friendships. Activities with friends take more work, and it is less complicated to simply stay home. Because of ease and accessibility, I have the tendency to stay put more now than in the past. Now, I enjoy the time spent alone, and I welcome being inside almost all the time.

A friend asked if I have felt left out of social situations since The Decline, to which I replied no. But this question is worth considering. In my small town, the city pool is a social hub in the summer, an attractive location especially for moms and their children. However, I no longer go there because of the heat and the difficulty in mobility. I no longer mingle in other social situations because of the hardship of moving around. Though my friends certainly give their best efforts to include me, I know they enjoy events in which I cannot participate because of the impossibility or difficulty of maneuverability. Though this is completely understandable, I do occasionally experience disappointment.

A good friend and I recently had the intention of eating lunch together at a local restaurant. The lengths she went to in order to avoid tall tables and stools, which do not work for me, was to her credit. When I was in the cane and walker stages, friends walked slowly with me. Now they take care to push me safely to ballpark bathrooms, push me through narrow doorways, lift my chair over door lips and curbs, rearrange furniture to make paths, carry my drink or trash, and run a variety of errands. They have let me put my full weight on them as I have climbed stairs, transferred seats, or simply taken a few steps. Friends like these are irreplaceable. I am forever grateful for their kindness and thoughtfulness regarding my disability, and I will never forget or overlook these acts.

I am determined to remain an involved and active wife, mom, and community member. Every time I attend school site council meetings, appointments, school activities, or community events, and my family isn't available to help, I must find someone to either transport me or get my wheelchair out of the van once I arrive. This takes organization and preparation, two qualities with which the Lord has gifted me. If a friend is not available to help, I have had to contact others I hardly know to get this accomplished. I find that anyone is happy to help, and it seems to create a bond between us. It also brings about awareness of disability difficulties; I have noted these helpers often have questions, realizations, or comments about accommodation specifics, particularly restroom and parking accessibility. I have rarely been in a situation where I needed help and it was hard for me to find.

> **"** *I have rarely been in a situation where I needed help and it was hard for me to find.*

On the other side of service, I hope I was just as helpful to others when I had the physical ability. Furnishing meals was previously a simple way for me to provide aid. This provision seems to be an easy way to help, but now knowing the benefit this is for my family, I realize it is vital.

Is there a sense of relief others feel when able to help? Are they learning about the details of disability? Even better, am I preparing my children or my friends' children for disability advocacy and activism?

I know the Lord is more concerned about service and the overall condition of my heart than the condition of my flesh. Though I would like for life to be the way I want it, this is a fleshly desire, and what I want doesn't matter. Life is not about me. Life is about the Lord's purposes, and it is necessary for the healthy condition of my heart to recognize these purposes and his provision in all situations.

Life is not about me.

The Lord is a provider.

Choosing to Love

By Debbie's husband Phil

We love because he first loved us.[1]

I can clearly remember sitting in the patient room at the neurologist office in Kansas City with Debbie and her parents in 1997. The consultation was about to begin, and we would be finding out the results of the spinal tap and other tests as they attempted to determine what was causing Debbie's health issues.

There were a number of pamphlets in the office, and as I read them, it became pretty clear that a second exacerbation would need to take place prior to being fully diagnosed with MS. The doctor came in and told Debbie the scan was clear, but he never mentioned anything about a second exacerbation.

As I sat there, it became very real. I thought about her parents and what might be going through their minds. I tried to put myself in their shoes and wondered what fears they too were facing. Did they wonder if I would continue to care for their daughter?

I thought about Debbie, who was my girlfriend at the time, and while there was great relief in what the doctor told her, deep down I knew. This journey was just beginning, and the biggest question I faced was whether or not I was going to be part of it.

You see, as a young boy growing up, I saw the devastation of this disease in the marriage of friends of my parents. The wife's MS was fast-paced and debilitating. This was a couple who loved the Lord; yet for some reason, the husband decided that the marriage vow no longer applied. It had a huge impact on me even as a little boy. How could someone say they love Jesus and then completely run away when things got tough?

I don't remember how much time transpired before the second exacerbation took place, but the memory of the doctor delivering the news that Debbie was officially diagnosed with MS is still very vivid and real. The hope that perhaps she would never fully be diagnosed was put to bed that day. I didn't know what to say, and I sure didn't know what to do, which seems to almost be an anthem of sorts in our journey. If anything positive came from the diagnosis, it was that so many of our questions and unknowns were eliminated. Except for one that would continue to linger.

A short time later, I went with Debbie and her parents to a presentation about the three MS medications on the market at the time. There was such a broad range of people there, young to old, male to female. Some had minor disabilities, and there was a young woman who appeared to be even younger than Debbie. I'll never forget her. She was married, but her husband was stationed overseas, and she was on her own at McConnell Air Force Base with nobody around to help her. She was already in need of a walker, and it was clear she had a long road ahead of her. I remember thinking, how long will it be before Debbie will be in this position? Might she be able to live a fairly normal life? Perhaps her case will be incredibly mild, like some of the other patients I saw in the room that day. Either way, the weight of the reality fully set in, and it became clear that I had an incredibly difficult decision to make.

I have never shared any of this with my wife or anyone else, so this is all pretty raw right now. Debbie and I dated for close to five years before I finally proposed and asked her to marry me. People had a lot of fun joking with us about this length of time, but I know it caused some pain for Debbie, those closest to her, and her parents. There were a few factors that contributed to this length of time, but at times, the "what ifs" were so hard to avoid and incredibly daunting to think about. The gravity of this decision, if I chose to stay with Debbie, made it not easy to make. Could I love her like Jesus loved the Bride?[2] Did I fully comprehend what I was signing up for?

Jesus loved Debbie just as she was. He saw his daughter going through this immense emotional pain, and his love for her never waned. Was I capable of this kind of love? Could I love her in her brokenness, just like Jesus did? How could I ever look Jesus in the eye and tell him I wasn't willing to love his daughter? What kind of man would I be if I refused to see her as he did, perfectly and wonderfully made in his image? He knit Debbie in the womb, just like he knit me![3]

I remember writing a letter to Debbie and giving it to her the night before we got married. One of the things I wanted to express in the letter was that I was choosing to love her. I had made the conscious decision to love her no matter what came our way, and it was at this point our journey together with Jesus began.

I've always had a deep love and respect for Debbie's parents, Tom and Miriam. Other than my own mother, I've never met anyone that loves Jesus as much as them. I saw the way they chased after Jesus as a married couple, and it inspired me and drew me to them. I saw firsthand what a godly biblical marriage should look like, and I'm forever grateful Jesus gave me that gift before my own marriage.

Husbands, love your wives, just as Christ loved the church and gave Himself up for her.[4]

On July 28, 2001, Debbie and I officially became Mr. and Mrs. Phil Oelke. We were humbled and honored to have Debbie's dad officiate the service. As he gave his message to us, I heard his heart loud and clear. There would be trials later on. How would I respond? Would I stay committed to his daughter and love her? I think in the back of our minds, we both knew what was to come.

I stood in front of our friends, family, and, most importantly, Jesus. I made my intentions known to everyone, and I took a vow that I would always love, cherish, and protect my bride, in sickness and in health. It sure seems those two words should be flipped around. In health *and* in sickness!

Ephesians 5:25 became one of my life verses that day. How thankful I am that Jesus himself loved me the same way, despite my own "disabilities," and showed me how to love and sacrifice for my bride.

I knew it wasn't going to be easy, but his word clearly states in Philippians 4:13, "I can do all this through him who gives me strength." This verse can be cliché for some, but I believe these words, and I praise Jesus because he has done exactly what he promised in that single, powerful sentence!

Then Jesus said to His disciples, "Whoever wants to be my disciple must deny themselves and take up their cross and follow me."[5]

I don't have any idea what our life is going to look like in the next few years, but I am so incredibly proud of and thankful for the bride Jesus gave me. Sacrificing for her is easy because she seeks Jesus every day! I look forward to loving Jesus together with my bride and praising him with hands lifted high!

CHAPTER 7

Jireh

> "O God, our help in ages past,
> Our hope for years to come,
> Our shelter from the stormy blast,
> And our eternal home."
>
> –Isaac Watts, *O God, Our Help in Ages Past*

The Lord tells us to consider it pure joy when we face trials.[1] Does the Lord's command to rejoice mean we need to be joyful about everything?

Because I don't always feel happiness. I'm not figuratively jumping for joy.

Because I don't always see the way out of this disability.

Does he really provide in every single situation? Does the promise mean he provides a way that avoids the situation and completely circumvents it? Or does his provision help us to pass through hardship with the least amount of angst?

Does this supply come in every situation? Or solely during the times the Lord deems challenging?

The Apostle Paul encourages us by saying, "But when you are tempted, he will also provide a way out so that you can endure it."[2] At least sixteen translations of *The Holy Bible* use the word "escape," reassuring us he is making a way for us to escape temptation. Among other definitions, this means to break free from confinement. Not being able to walk and therefore being in a wheelchair is quite confining to me. I would gratefully accept a way of escape, a way to break free. But my way of escape, which would be to walk, apparently is not the same as the Lord's view of escape.

> **❝** *Not being able to walk and therefore being in a wheelchair is quite confining to me. I would gratefully accept a way of escape, a way to break free.*

Even the names of the Lord in Scripture refer to his qualities of providing a way out of hardship. The names of the Lord in Hebrew capture my attention, as I like to keep them clear in mind. YHWH (Yahweh) and Jehovah are more appropriate than the word God because most religions call their supreme being "god." A Hebrew name, Jehovah Jireh, means "The LORD will provide," and was first established as a location in Genesis 22. This chapter holds the only instance of the word Jireh being used in the Bible. In the Book of Genesis, Jehovah Jireh, or Yahweh Yireh, was the location of the binding of Isaac, where Yahweh told Abraham to offer his son Isaac as a burnt offering. Abraham named the place Jireh after the Lord provided a ram to sacrifice in place of Isaac.

It doesn't even make sense to be asked to cause the ultimate loss, the loss of life. The fact that Abraham was asked to take the life of his son, who was the result of a miraculous birth and the promised start of the Lord's people, is unfathomable.

Even more so is Abraham's obedience to the Lord. He had total faith the Lord would provide. That's blind trust! I hope to have the same blind trust and faith. When Jesus tells us his Father only gives good gifts[3], then the converse must also be true: he does not give bad gifts. No matter what I think the cause and purpose of my multiple sclerosis is, the truth tells me he gives good gifts.

In the midst of my losses, I have seen the Lord's gifts and provision.

My oldest son has echoed this as his primary lesson about the Lord through this experience, learning for certain the Lord will provide. While complete healing is always and forever my first desire, the Lord is undeniably taking care of my family through this difficult time. His care for my family is so thorough that my twelve-year-old son has even stated he doesn't think he experiences any challenges from my disability. Thank the Lord for his words!

Approximately one month before I moved to a wheelchair full-time, we bought an electric motorized wheelchair. I entered this search and eventual purchase reluctantly, likely because I thought I wouldn't need it soon. I am an eternal optimist. I had the assumption I would not get to "that point" so soon. But the Lord knew otherwise, and he put it on my husband's heart to explore mobility options. Besides the fact that I do not have the lower body strength, balance, or coordination to *not* use the chair, I also don't have the upper body strength to maneuver a traditional wheelchair throughout my house during the day. Thank the Lord for this motorized chair!

In early May 2021, we moved our bedroom upstairs to the main level of our house, trading bedrooms with our oldest son, which gave him the master suite in the basement.

The room with the large walk-in closet.

The room with the attached bathroom.

The room I had lovingly decorated and arranged, thoroughly enjoying our very own retreat.

Though it seems to be a minor loss in comparison with the progressing disability, to give up our expansive room and closet was a challenge. However, conveniently, our "new" bedroom is right next to the main bathroom, which I am using as my primary bathroom for the first time since moving into the house nine years ago. Thank the Lord for rooms easily accessible during the day!

Within weeks of moving upstairs and being in a wheelchair full-time, I experienced a more sudden and rapid decline. I began to experience almost complete foot drop on the left side and was not able to move well in bed. Though it is typically uncomfortable for me, I immediately got accustomed to sleeping on my back. I was no longer able to independently move in and out of the shower or even the bathroom as a whole. We had a regular and pre-scheduled teleconference with my neurologist during this scary time. This appointment had been scheduled six months before. Thank the Lord for his timing!

" Within weeks of moving upstairs and being in a wheelchair full-time, I experienced a more sudden and rapid decline.

This teleconference altered the direction of The Decline. My neurologist suggested an immediate five-day course of one-hour-long IV steroid infusions. These infusions made an enormous difference. It was indeed life changing as it altered the development of my disease. After the series of steroids, I could pick up my left foot and walk in my inaccessible bathroom, I could turn over in bed, and I could shower independently. I was pleasantly surprised to see I had a bit of mobility in my left foot and toes. These amazing, miraculous improvements continue! Thank the Lord for steroids!

During the week of very limited movement, a friend of ours offered to financially support the widening of our upstairs bathroom door to make it handicap accessible. Though this is no longer necessary, it was completed in preparation of whatever the future holds. Thank the Lord for loving friends!

When I was nearing drop foot I looked into some sort of ankle boot or brace so I could move around the house by myself. I mentioned this search to my parents, and my father nonchalantly said my grandmother (his stepmother) no longer wanted to use the anti-foot drop "boot" she had for her Parkinson's Disease. It had not been inexpensive. Though within a week I didn't need it because of the steroid infusion, all of a sudden, I had an ankle-foot orthotic boot to use! Thank the Lord for a casual mention!

During that time, a friend who is an amateur photographer called to offer a photo session. Because she was a new friend who lived some distance away, she was completely unaware of our situation. This shoot was a needed respite from the realities of our current and ongoing challenges. When looking at the pictures, one cannot ascertain they were taken during a very challenging time of life. We need to feel like a regular family. We need to do things other families do. We need normalization. Though having a mother in a wheelchair is now normal for my children, Phil and I are very familiar with life without a disability. We miss that life. In our new normal, we need to increasingly become accustomed to life with a disability. Thank the Lord for causing others to unknowingly give us exactly what we needed! Thank the Lord for our friend's obedience!

> " *Phil and I are very familiar with life without a disability. We miss that life. In our new normal, we need to increasingly become accustomed to life with a disability.*

A conversation I approached with apprehension was one I needed to have with my naturopath. Generally, there seems to be a conflict between natural, alternative treatments and conventional medicine. Because of this, I was uneasy about re-entering the traditional medical world and I wondered if I could somehow merge the two differing opinions, similar to combining two rivals. Thankfully, my naturopath, with whom I had been working for eight months, had a flexible attitude and was significantly supportive of this re-entry into the medical world. Because of the rapid decline, a steroid infusion and beginning a DMT for multiple sclerosis were necessary. Thank the Lord for my naturopath's easygoing response!

A longtime friend of my husband offered to weld a ramp that would accommodate my wheelchair from the back door into the backyard. I could now sit at our patio table. I could now watch the kids play in the backyard. Thank the Lord for selfless giving!

When we were having mechanical trouble with my van, a relatively new friend spent countless hours working on it until it was drivable. The details of the complex and seemingly tangled wires were more than I needed to know. I do not have the mental capacity for or interest in the details. Thank the Lord for gifting friends with intricate knowledge!

A longtime favorite verse of mine is Psalm 139:5a, "You hem me in behind and before." I have wondered the specifics of this—how he hems me in before I speak words I may regret, before I travel places, or before I do something for which I need to repent. But I then saw evidence of being hemmed in. Last semester, my kids' fourth-grade class had a COVID-19 outbreak. At the outset, this was extremely unwelcome news because another student's mother, who was a close friend of mine, was going out of town to help her own newly widowed mother after surgery. This friend's fourth-grade son was declared negative for COVID-19 three separate times, which more than gave her the clearance she needed to assist her mother in recovery. This knowledge was necessary for the caretaking. Thank the Lord for his promise to go ahead of us!

Several more instances of provision are apparent during this time, as we have been the recipients of countless financial gifts, notes, texts, letters, cards, and prayers. Grandma Luella's direct descendants have especially done so notably. Thank the Lord for his generous work through others!

Standing firm on the Lord's character and his promises has become essential; however, this stance takes consistent and disciplined work. Though I do not literally stand, I will continue to figuratively rise up in the Lord. Reading the word of the Lord teaches me about his character and his promises. Written thousands of years ago, the Lord shows me how to stand:

> " *Though I do not literally stand, I will continue to figuratively rise up in the Lord.*

"I know that my redeemer lives, and that in the end he will stand on the earth." Job 19:25

"It is for freedom that Christ has set us free. Stand firm, then, and do not let yourselves be burdened again by a yoke of slavery." Galatians 5:1

"Be on your guard; stand firm in the faith; be courageous; be strong." 1 Corinthians 16:13

"But our citizenship is in heaven. And we eagerly await a Savior from there, the Lord Jesus Christ, who, by the power that enables him to bring everything under his control, will transform our lowly bodies so that they will be like his glorious body. Therefore, my brothers and sisters, you whom I love and long for, my joy and crown, stand firm in the Lord in this way, dear friends!" Philippians 3:20-4:1

"So then, brothers and sisters, stand firm and hold fast to the teachings we passed on to you, whether by word of mouth or by letter." 2 Thessalonians 2:15

"Finally, be strong in the Lord and in his mighty power. Put on the full armor of God, so that you can take your stand against the devil's schemes. For our struggle is not against flesh and blood, but against the rulers, against the authorities, against the powers of this dark world and against the spiritual forces of evil in the heavenly realms. Therefore put on the full armor of God, so that when the day of evil comes, you may be able to stand your ground, and after you have done everything, to stand. Stand firm then, with the belt of truth buckled around your waist, with the breastplate of righteousness in place, and with your feet fitted with the readiness that comes from the gospel of peace. In addition to all this, take up the shield of faith, with which you can extinguish all the flaming arrows of the evil one. Take the helmet of salvation and the sword of the Spirit, which is the word of God." Ephesians 6:10-17

"The LORD said to Joshua, 'Stand up!'" Joshua 7:10a

After learning to stand strong in the Lord, I resolved to not be shaken, moved, or deterred by my circumstances:

"I keep my eyes always on the LORD. With him at my right hand, I will not be shaken." Psalm 16:8

"Therefore, since we are receiving a kingdom that cannot be shaken, let us be thankful, and so worship God acceptably with reverence and awe." Hebrews 12:28

"Truly he is my rock and my salvation; he is my fortress, I will never be shaken." Psalm 62:2

"For the king trusts in the LORD; through the unfailing love of the Most High, he will not be shaken." Psalm 21:7

As steadfast and unshaken as I am, I still get very hopeful for full physical healing when I read about the Lord's provision, "I will repay you for the years the locusts have eaten…"[4] A friend placed this verse on a notecard in her vehicle for years, and wonderfully this "repayment" has happened in her life. She now enjoys a wonderful marriage after her first one ended because of infidelity and abuse. I would love Jehovah Jireh to provide my own years of restoration. I occasionally want to beg the Lord to "Give us gladness in proportion to our former misery! Replace the evil years with good."[5] These years may seem to me to be miserable and evil, but then I read, "When I said, 'My foot is slipping,' your unfailing love, LORD, supported me."[6] My own feet have slipped often, especially in the cane and walker stages, and it would often result in a fall. But a physical support probably isn't what is intended here. The psalm continues, "When anxiety was great within me, your consolation brought me joy."[7] Though I certainly have had anxiety through The Decline, having the Lord's joy needs to be enough of a provision for me. The Lord himself needs to be fully satisfying for me. He is enough. The Lord *does* provide for me. It's more proof of his love than I need.

> " *The Lord himself needs to be fully satisfying for me. He is enough. The Lord* does *provide for me. It's more proof of his love than I need.*

My family certainly recognizes these proofs along with me. But they are the people with whom I do life the most. I am *still* determining the effect of my disability on being a wife and mom. Does my life show evidence of the Lord's deep, unfathomable love and constant provision?

His deep, unfathomable love certainly continued. His love was further proved in a chapter of our life that is unparalleled.

Cottonwood.

Remembering the Meaningful

By Debbie's friend Carisa

Debbie and I have been friends for more than twenty years. We started out as two bright-eyed young women who ended up working for the same school district. We became fast friends bonding over shared experiences with students, similar interests, and faith. We drove to work together on days we were at the same school, and gradually began spending more time together outside of school. We have spent hours combing the countryside of Kansas looking for out-of-the-way antique shops, hoping to find that one special piece to add to our various collections. During our summers off, we frequently got together for coffee or smoothies. We ran two half-marathons together, and for years, we ran a shared business featuring vintage items.

I'm not sure when it started, but Tuesday mornings became our mornings to work out together. At different times we ran, walked, and in 2013 we even attempted to "walk" our puppies. Our workouts always involved lots of sharing—things that were good, things that were hard, and how we could pray for each other. We adjusted our workouts at times when each of us was pregnant, and later we adjusted as Debbie's health began to decline. At first, we just shortened our route and then as walking became more difficult, we even changed to Debbie riding her bike with me walking. Neither of us was willing to give up on this time together, and Debbie's positive and determined spirit really came through. She physically pushed herself in order to maintain as much mobility as possible, and she did not complain when it was difficult.

Neither of us was a stranger to adversity. Our journey as friends had included health issues, infertility, and grief over loss of loved ones, but this was a new kind of loss. Watching a close friend lose mobility and independence is not something you expect to deal with. I vividly remember Debbie sharing with our coworkers that she had been diagnosed with MS, but honestly, I never pictured this course of events.

I think for me, the hardest thing has been a feeling of helplessness. I can make myself available to rearrange and organize cupboards, cook a meal, or get groceries. Those things are easy. What's harder is making sense of a difficulty like this in someone so young. What's harder is staying faithful to pray and not giving up hope. I had my daughter hand letter a verse for me—it serves as a reminder to stay hopeful. It's in my hallway and I pass it multiple times a day: "I remain confident of this: I will see the goodness of the LORD in the land of the living. Wait for the LORD; be strong and take heart and wait for the LORD."[1] I know there are ways Debbie is experiencing the goodness of the Lord right now while she is here on earth—she shares testimonies about God's goodness and his faithfulness all the time. Even though she hasn't been healed as we would like her to be, her story is one of hope. Her faithfulness and her attitude of hope is contagious. I'm proud of the way she freely talks about the ups and downs, and I'm challenged by the grace with which she faces adversity.

CHAPTER 8

Cottonwood

> "If you examine your life well, you will
> find many instances when God showed his
> unmistakable mercy to you.
> Trouble was brewing, but it passed you by
> for some reason. God delivered you.
> Acknowledge these and thank God, who
> loves you."
>
> –Theophan the Recluse

Unmistakable mercy? Does that mean this time of life is a blessing in disguise?

Cottonwood, an experience so significant it deserves its own space.

The year 2020 is infamous. It's known as a difficult year of pandemic, vaccines, and mask choices or mandates. A year of quarantines, online meetings, and homeschooling. Sometimes we had to hunt for hidden blessings, other times we did not.

The obvious blessings were enjoying increased family time and discovering new outdoor activities. We liked spending time together, and many made-up games, indoor and out, became more and more prominent as the year wore on.

But then, in the late summer, we wondered about the direction life was taking us. We wondered about the Lord's purposes. It was discovered some of our most-used basement rooms had mold. Was this detection a hidden blessing? It wasn't obvious at first to our family.

> **"** *Sometimes we had to hunt for hidden blessings, other times we did not.*

However, we should have known the outcome would be amazing.

Wisdom and joy come after pressing times. Gold has to be heated to be purified. Rainbows appear after storms. Grapes must undergo pressure in order to become wine. Muscles need to tear in order to become bigger. Cacao beans are bitter, but after drying and roasting, they eventually form chocolate.

Wonderful results occur through trials.

Our trial, mold, was predominantly in the master bedroom of our house as well as my office. There is a possible connection between mold and multiple sclerosis; toxic mold can cause chronic inflammatory responses and mold is a toxicant that causes nerve damage associated with MS. Because of this possible connection, the affected walls had to be torn down, rebuilt, and protected. This meant it was necessary for us to temporarily move out of the house because we did not have enough bedroom or bathroom space for five people upstairs in the ground level of our home. We didn't even know the extent of the mold—whether the upstairs was affected or not. We had no place to go.

Then "unmistakable mercy" fell in our laps.

Like a river in a desert.

Like a phoenix rising from ashes.

Like sight to one that was blind.

Like a sliver of light in the darkest of caves.

> " *Then 'unmistakable mercy' fell in our laps.*

A kindred friend graciously offered the use of his own family's country retreat. And this was no hut in the woods, but rather an expansive, eighty-acre riverfront property with a home less than three years old. It had been known as his family's fishing "cabin," nicknamed Cottonwood for the winding river through the property and the trees that swished up and down its banks. Though twenty-two miles away from our hometown, we immediately moved to Cottonwood and called it our home for five months. We fell in love with the wraparound porch, the "beach" on the bank of the river, acres to explore, and wildflowers to enjoy. Our contentment continued with a hot tub and deep black nights that made stars easy to identify. We watched many different wildlife species roam the property, either passing through or calling the acreage home. A bald eagle, golden eagle, bobcat, armadillo, whitetail deer, and gray fox enjoyed the land with us. The distance from town and endless opportunities to roam were wonderful excuses to stay home as our family enjoyed seemingly unending time together. Learning to operate a riding lawnmower and pulling a sled through snow behind a utility terrain vehicle (UTV) were new adventures.

In the walker stage at the time, I spent hours on the porch while my family was in school, dubbing myself a "recluse with Jesus." Sitting in the expansive outdoor living area, having a choice between rocking chairs and a wicker couch, I was consumed by doing nothing but enjoying the Lord's character and his amazing palette in nature.

Less than a week after we moved into Cottonwood, I underwent a quick and painless stem cell replacement procedure that had the purpose of replacing harmful cells in my body with my own unused stem cells. Several friends gathered the day before to pray for the FDA-unapproved method. This memorable and special moment instigated one of them coming to Cottonwood to pray over the property, particularly to pray for my family's safety.

Growing up in the city, I had a long-held fear of living "in the country." My overactive imagination could draw up many unrealistic scenarios involving dangerous intruders. This dread would now be difficult to control because of the wide-open feel of Cottonwood; I had to conquer it. My alarm was irrational, and it was a worry from which I needed release. The fear didn't make sense. When we had moved to Cottonwood, I genuinely and fully believed the stem cell procedure would heal me, so why would I doubt the Lord would not keep my family safe at Cottonwood?

But extinguishing this fear was quite challenging for me; I would not be victorious without the Lord's help. Because the

Lord's perfect love for me drives out fear[1], and because fear is the opposite of faith, I knew trust was required.

Cottonwood had an alarm system and the home even had security cameras. During the first weeks there, when home alone, I regularly set the alarm because it made me feel safe. However, for me, setting this alarm was not a display of trust. Frustrated with myself for having a nonsensical fear, I remembered, "Some trust in chariots and some in horses, but we trust in the name of the LORD our God."[2] I needed to fully believe God's word. That he offered sufficient provision for my safety. That he was enough for me. But I needed his help to get rid of this fear; I was not able to extinguish it on my own. He gave me what I needed, and my fear soon dissipated. To prove it, the alarm was disarmed for the remainder of our stay.

> " *I needed his help to get rid of this fear;*
> *I was not able to extinguish it on my own.*

Friends enjoyed coming to visit the beautiful home and property; a girlfriend even brought fresh flowers on her first visit. We were very surprised when over thirty friends gathered at this hard-to-find and out-of-the-way property to sing Christmas carols. Another friend drove wildly on the "mule" UTV, finding wild gourds with me in order to decorate for the fall. UTVs are said to be used more for work than recreation, but we certainly were entertained by the reverse. My family both made and discovered many trails through the property, enjoying every new and old path.

My mother-in-law and parents loved coming to visit, and Beth even came for a long weekend with her family. Living "in the country" was a new experience for most of them, and they quickly saw the advantages. My kids easily found adventures, discovering hedge apples, fish bones, deer carcasses, clamshells, and many different types of native grasses and wild berries on "our" acreage. Unexpectedly celebrating both Thanksgiving and Christmas at our temporary home created precious memories, including cutting down a Christmas tree. Within an hour, we experienced "cedar fever," and promptly set the tree outside!

Though I adored our experience in the country, there were some things about living in town I missed. I missed my home, my kitchen, and the close conveniences. I had relished groceries being carried to my vehicle without being asked, waving to passersby, and talking to neighbors. I missed the local post office knowing to forward mislabeled mail to our newer address of over nine years. I missed the frequent interaction with both strangers and friends. Wondering if I could ever live in the country on a permanent basis led me to realize the balance between the pros and cons was difficult to reconcile.

During our absence, the prescribed mold remediation at our home revealed issues that became worse and worse. The problems accumulated and seemed never-ending. Just when we thought we couldn't take any more, something additional would go wrong with our home. The mold removal involved tearing out parts of walls, trim, and flooring. This led to the discovery of foundation issues that were more major and extensive than expected. After the house was professionally sturdied, the sewer backed up twice, a water line broke, and we experienced a long delay as we waited for carpet to arrive. Electrical problems tested our courage. Cost of materials skyrocketed because of COVID-19 as our patience and resolve wore thin.

We certainly thought we had plenty to deal with already. In the meantime, The Decline still progressed.

Living on rural acreage on a permanent basis became more and more attractive.

～～～

But the Lord never wastes tough times, or any experiences for that matter. We looked for his providence and proof of love through the challenges.

> *"But the Lord never wastes tough times, or any experiences for that matter.*

Sunrises, sunsets, and other magnificent displays of nature were obvious ways the Lord proved his love for us. The beauty of the changing seasons was further evidence. The trees of the field did clap their hands[3], and the rocks did cry out[4]! The night skies were clear. "The heavens declare the glory of God; the skies proclaim the work of his hands. Day after day they pour forth speech; night after night they reveal knowledge. They have no speech, they use no words; no sound is heard from them."[5]

In late January 2021, it was with extreme bittersweet feelings that we finished our major remodeling well enough to move back into our "real" home, and we said goodbye to Cottonwood.

Our family of five is forever changed, and we often discuss our experience at Cottonwood with longing.

We want to have birthday gatherings and respite weekends there.

We want to relive fun experiences there.

We want to drive the mule, allow our dog to roam freely, and go for walks completely surrounded by the Lord's creation.

The end of our time there was over, and the end of a tumultuous year came more quickly than we desired. In all these transitions, the Lord reminded me in Isaiah 45:

He summoned me by name.

He would send good times and bad times.

He would bring prosperity and create disaster.

He would speak only what is true.

He would never go back on his word.

He would not have told me to seek him if he could not be found.

He made the world to live in, not to be a place of empty chaos.

Because he is the Lord, and there is no other.

Fortunately, he is everywhere and needs no invitation to continue to play an integral role in our lives. During our Cottonwood experience, we had learned lessons that would stay with us through the next set of difficulties.

We learned through the challenges, as we continued life without physical healing, the Lord would be with us.

Expecting to Overcome

By Debbie's friend Alaina

How do you judge someone who has been given a tremendous burden to bear? I prefer not to, and yet we as humans are quick to compare and categorize. Part of me wants to hide from the pain, the other part wants to glean wisdom and strength moment by moment. Am I judging as I watch one's struggles, or is it learning? Is it really appropriate to call it a burden, or is it maybe a gift? I do not know the answer to these questions, but the more I am around Debbie, the more I see the need to press into the questions, press into the pain, press into the burden-gift.

I met Debbie through our husbands. My husband Jeff attended a men's retreat in January of 2016 with Phil, Debbie's husband. They connected through the Holy Spirit, and I was soon encouraged to attend a partnering women's ministry event to see what it was all about. Debbie was one of the speakers that weekend, and I remember thinking she had everything together. Her talk was flawless and matter of fact. There were no questions left hanging, and she used Scripture all throughout. It was evident she spent a lot of time with the Lord. I wondered how she could ever need anything from or be drawn to someone like me.

One of the first times we spent time together was when I took my daughter to play with her kids at the pool. I sat down by the edge of the pool, and she told me she couldn't feel much from her waist down any more. I remember where we were sitting, that Debbie had a black swimsuit on, and I wondered how much one could do without feeling in their lower extremities. She was still walking on her own and driving fine, so life must not be too different, right? We continued to get together to go shopping at vintage stores, eat out, get coffee, and spend time together at each other's houses every couple months or so. Since that day, life *has* become very different for Debbie.

I listened as she debated different forms of treatments and diets. I prayed with her as she sought healing through prayer and continue to pray with her weekly about whatever is happening in our lives. We started this about a year and a half ago, and I am honored to be a part of her life in a way that she shares these hard things with me.

I watched as she progressed to using a cane and how hard that was for her. Then came the walker, and she would use it to sit down and rest now and then as we were perusing aisles of clothes. This was about the time she needed to take naps in the afternoon, so she would sleep while I drove us home. She was still able to get through most antique stores with her walker, so neither one of these slowed us down too much. And now she has the motorized scooter. Yes, it is more cumbersome to get in and out of vehicles, but also useful for hanging shopping items on. No, we can't go to every store we used to, but she is able to go farther with the scooter. There are now more things I need to assist her with, but being able to help Debbie in this way makes me feel useful, like I have something to offer. I know she would say my friendship is offer enough, but I can't describe the feeling of being able to do something for her like steady her as she gets into her seat, lifting the scooter into the back of the van (I enjoy physical labor!), driving her hours and hours so we can go to a craft fair or flea market, helping her get to the toilet because the bathroom isn't handicap accessible, and picking her up off my hall floor because my house isn't handicap accessible. These things seem base and negligible, and yet, they mean a lot to me, both the good and the bad.

Through all the pressing into the questions and the pain, the way I have seen Debbie grow is in what I would describe as an emotional softening. As I said when I first heard her speak, it seemed as though she had everything together. I wanted to spend more time with her because I had been praying for someone to mentor me, and I wanted to see what was underneath. In struggling through this disease, I have seen Debbie move from undesirous of showing emotion to more and more being okay with crying with me. This has come about by her pressing into the questions! And it has taught me more than any words could.

So, if I judge, then I judge thus: crying and sharing pain is healing. Emotion comes when we are at the end of ourselves, and our heart finally catches up with our head. God is our provider, and we are utterly dependent on him. And if I have learned anything from her, then I have learned that vulnerability is a gift we give to each other. It can't be one-sided. If Jesus came as a baby, he must be okay with it too.

CHAPTER 9

But If Not

"When Jesus landed and saw a large crowd,
he had compassion on them and healed
their sick."

–Matthew 14:14

Do miraculous, unexplainable healings still happen today?

I would desperately love to be healed. I'm talking about physical healing. I know there has been some healing going on spiritually in me, which truly is irreplaceable, but I want physical healing. Sooner rather than later.

Sooner than when my children would prefer to spend time with peers than their mother. Sooner than the possibility of my upper body weakening more. Sooner than when my kids graduate and get married. Sooner than when I have grandkids and want to play on the floor with them.

Soon being the operative word. As in *my* definition of soon. But the Lord defines it differently. A family favorite miniseries about the ministry of Jesus envisions a conversation between the characters regarding the timing of "soon." It is said that the word is quite imprecise. No one knows the meaning, whether it is a few hours, a few days, many years, one hundred years, or even one thousand years. This projected conversation is referring to a statement in Psalm 90:4, which compares one thousand years to one day. Peter repeats this concept, "But do not forget this one thing, dear friends: With the Lord a day is like a thousand years, and a thousand years are like a day."[1] My twenty years of asking for healing doesn't even compare to one thousand. My twenty years, though extremely painful, are like a quick snap to the Lord. Like a blip on radar. Like a piece of sand in the ocean.

> **"** *I know there has been some healing going on spiritually in me, which truly is irreplaceable, but I want physical healing.*

But his thoughts about me outnumber those tiny bits.[2]

And he has heard my thoughts and musings. I know this for certain.

Nevertheless, I haven't been healed. It isn't for a lack of countless, sincere prayers. It's not for a lack of heartfelt individual and group prayers.

I haven't been healed after being anointed with oil or after praying for deliverance.

I haven't been healed after being prayed for by those who have the gift of healing, both those well-known and those lesser-known.

I haven't been healed where Jesus himself healed others.

I haven't been healed through many tears, countless periods of weeping, and multiple silent groans.

I haven't been healed by digging up and repenting of every known sin.

I'm still disabled.

In the meantime, I am going to live life.

History is full of people who embraced life after experiencing a trial. Tough times didn't dissuade them. Vincent van Gogh still painted. Nancy Kerrigan still ice skated. Bethany Hamilton still surfed. Jesus still came back to life for us, and he will forever be our resurrection.

> **"***In the meantime, I am going to live life.***

Even if I am not physically healed, I am still going to continue to pursue any ministry the Lord might have for me. At a recent conference, when I told my hopes for ministry to a woman who was praying for my healing, she pointed to my wheelchair and asked, "In that?"

Yes, in this.

In this confining wheelchair.

In this source of never-ending grief.

In this lack of physical strength.

But also in this profusion of mighty spiritual power. Also in this joy that comes after mourning and in the morning.

The Lord says, "Go in the strength you have..."[3] My strength is minimal, but I can and will still be a part of furthering his kingdom.

I refuse to lament the fact that I have not been healed. I refuse to be sad and depressed about living in a wheelchair.

Life goes on.

I do not have the luxury of simply sitting around, being disappointed. I have three kids who need a mom who is as active in their lives as she always has been. Yes, this means our daily activities look a lot different now, but we still do life. We still go to the library, go to birthday parties, and go to friends' houses to hang out or play. I am still going to sit on my front porch and talk to my neighbors. I am still going to shop, go for coffee, and visit my friends. I am still going to host weekly moms' prayer meetings, whose members have witnessed The Decline.

Yes, it takes longer for my family to go anywhere because of my wheelchair use.

Yes, I need someone to get my more lightweight, easily transportable wheelchair out of the back of the vehicle when I arrive at my destination.

Yes, I need someone to push my wheelchair.

However, I have to act as if this is very normal. Because it is normal for our family.

> *I have to act as if this is very normal.*
> *Because it is normal for our family.*

During the summer, we are still going to get the same snow cones, ice cream, and frozen drinks as we typically would. I may not be able to go to the swimming pool anymore, but I am definitely going to ask friends to take my kids. We will play modified versions of outdoor games and all sorts of creatively engineered indoor ball games. We will still play heated games of chess and go on family walks. We will still have outdoor fires and make s'mores. We will still go see a movie, go on summer vacation, go to kids' athletic events, and go to school happenings.

I will continue to exercise. Despite previously running every morning and completing two half-marathons and a handful of 5K races, I have never loved long-distance runs. Though I would love to do it now, obviously I cannot, so I will enjoy sleeping a little later. I will find different ways to live a healthy lifestyle and stay active. This may mean doing the exercises suggested by my physical therapist, or it may mean riding my modified three-wheeled recumbent bike. It may mean "going for a walk" with my family while I ride in my motorized wheelchair, or it may mean spending the time necessary to build finger muscles so I can at least scribble my signature on a check. Life looks very different from the norm, and I desperately wish it was what it used to be, but this is normal for us. Our new normal.

Does this mean I have accepted living a life of disability?

Does this mean it is alright to be disabled?

To copy the popular game, "Would You Rather," would I rather live life in a wheelchair, trying to be as obedient as possible to the Lord, or be able to walk unhindered, far from being obedient to the Lord? Would I rather be home during the school day, spending time with the Lord, or be shopping all day, distracted by material goods?

I still pray for and desire healing, but while I wait, I am going to pursue obedience. I am not going to idly sit around. I will make the most of this time.

I will "bloom where I am planted." The Lord told the people of Israel right before being exiled to Babylon to prosper during their time of captivity. In enemy territory. He told them to build, settle, plant, eat, marry, and increase in number. He commanded his chosen people to seek peace and prosperity right in the enemy's camp. The Lord continued to encourage them to pray for the city of their captivity. He said, "Pray to the LORD for it, because if it prospers, you too will prosper."[4] He was commanding the refugees to pray for their oppressors! The community organized, maintained, and governed by the antagonist was to prosper! If it did indeed prosper, the Lord promised that his people, the Jews, would also thrive.[5]

What does this mean for me? If prosper and thrive mean to cause to succeed, then I most certainly will bloom during this time.

What does this mean for you?

I will seek to obey how the Lord wants me to live my life. I believe this means genuinely showing obvious joy and hope despite my circumstances.

This most certainly includes continuing one-on-one discipleship. These relationships have been meaningful to me over the years, as I have learned through mistakes and successes how to encourage women to strongly move forward and grow in their intimacy with the Lord. Meeting with these women and having a prime seat to their love relationships with the Lord is irreplaceable. Learning to be thoroughly see-through regarding life's turn of events, positive or negative, has been useful and necessary. Hopefully watching The Decline has been a tangible example of living in obedience to the Lord.

Following the Lord's leading also resulted in participating (through a different capacity) in an international women's ministry which emphasizes freedom in the Lord. Involvement with this ministry has been a major part of my life in the last decade. Previously, both pre-disability and while using a cane and then a walker, I was privileged to hold a leadership position and speak regularly. Whether it was teaching about topics related to freedom or giving a personal testimony, I spoke openly about my disease. Though the Lord led me away from that ministry two years ago, a return to it might be in my future. The ministry is, without doubt, a marvelous way to proclaim the Lord's goodness, both with words and actions. Using a disability aid at the weekend events has brought about unmatched connection with event attendees and opens many opportunities for genuine displays of candor.

Obedience may also include a new initiative that involves ministering to those experiencing any manner of loss. Details of this ministry are still in the works, but both my husband and I feel called to it. Through both successes and mistakes, we have learned considerably about loss and how to grieve well while still giving glory to Jesus Christ. We have the desire to convey hope while being transparent about failures and successes. While we have indeed struggled in this learning process, and we certainly still are, we feel led to share both our struggles and our joys in order to assist others in finding contentment amidst trials.

> **"** *We have the desire to convey hope while being transparent about failures and successes.*

All of these opportunities look very different now compared to the past, but perhaps that is what the Lord was working to accomplish all this time. Maybe he wanted me to be in this humble condition because he knew I could minister to others in ways better than ever!

I *always* want to be healed. Let there be no question about that absolute truth. But because I use a wheelchair, I have grown accustomed to being prayed over for the purpose of healing. I seem to be a magnet for these requests. I greatly appreciate these appeals to the Lord's throne, but because prayers for healing happen regularly, I admit I sometimes do not always focus on the words of intercession. My mind may wander with other thoughts and questions. Sometimes, it even seems as if I am calloused by the Lord answering these prayers in a way I don't understand. I am weary of not comprehending his answers though I know I can't yet see the Lord's ways of doing things. It's easy to express this trust, but harder to put into practice. When people look at me toward the end of a prayer and ask if I feel any differently, I often feel guilty for being in the same physical condition. While I completely appreciate and agree with their expectation of healing, the answer has always been "No."

Though we personally don't see the results we would have hoped for by the end of the prayer, disappointment does not deter me. Early followers of "The Way" were also surprised and disappointed that fellow Christians experienced illness and death. In the book of 1 Thessalonians, Paul devotes time to this question: how are Christians to understand death? The Thessalonians may have been confused when members of their community fell sick and passed away before Christ's promised return. Paul's words of hope in the face of sorrow and tragedy are commonly read at funerals and memorial services even today: "Brothers and sisters, we do not want you to be uninformed about those who sleep in death, so that you do not grieve like the rest of mankind, who have no hope. For we believe that Jesus died and rose again, and so we believe that God will bring with Jesus those who have fallen asleep in him."[6]

Beginning in the latter part of the first century, Christians in Rome, among other places, were buried in underground cemeteries called catacombs. Catacombs were built outside city walls because of laws forbidding burial within city limits. These below-ground tunnels offered privacy, respite from authorities, and the opportunity to freely use Christian symbols, one of the earliest being an anchor. Others were the cross and the fish.

The idea of an anchor as a metaphor for steadfastness in the Lord originated with the writer of Hebrews, who said, "We have this hope as an anchor for the soul, firm and secure."[7] This symbol of hope is equated with steadfastness, calm, and composure. Just as steadfastness means standing firm, I stand firm on the Lord. I will continue to cling to my anchor.

> **❝** *I stand firm on the Lord. I will continue to cling to my anchor.*

⊱⋆⊰

When Shadrach, Meshach, and Abednego were about to be thrown into the fiery furnace, their response to King Nebuchadnezzar was, "...the God we serve is able to deliver us...But even if he does not, we want you to know, Your Majesty, that we will not serve your gods..."[8] Nebuchadnezzar had become king of Babylon in 605 BC and is historically known as Nebuchadnezzar the Great. In an effort aimed at stopping Egypt from gaining a foothold, he destroyed the land of Judah, including the city of Jerusalem and Solomon's temple, in 586 BC. This destruction led to the Hebrew captivity, as Judah's citizens were deported to Babylon. Daniel 3 details the statue King Nebuchadnezzar erected of himself, which explains his extreme anger at the refusal of Shadrach, Meshach, and Abednego to bow down and worship it. They were resolved to obey the Lord and refused to bow down to anything but the

One, True God whether he chose to save them or not. They knew he wasn't obligated to help them.

Their refusal, as well as their words, "But if not..." are quite notable and memorable. These words were instantly recognizable in 1940 to the people who were accustomed to hearing the Bible read in church. They knew the story of Shadrach, Meshach, and Abednego told in the book of Daniel. Because they recognized this phrase, the desperate message in those three little words was clear to Allied commanders.

In the summer of 1940, hundreds of thousands of Allied soldiers were trapped at Dunkirk, France. Enemy German forces heading their direction planned to destroy them. It would take a miracle to save the Allied powers! The potential catastrophe seemed hopeless because they were determined not to surrender. When all appeared lost, a British naval officer sent a telegraph to London that contained three words of hope, "But if not." This simple three-word phrase communicated desperation and resolve at the same time. When it seemed certain the Allied forces at Dunkirk were about to be destroyed, the Axis powers hesitated. It is not known why they briefly backed off, but what happened next is known as the Miracle of Dunkirk. British families and fishermen across the English Channel heard about the cry for help, and they answered with a variety of smaller vessels—merchant marine boats, pleasure cruisers, and even small fishing boats. By a miracle of the Lord, within ten days, Allied forces' military destroyers and hundreds of smaller civilian boats evacuated more than 338,000 soldiers and took them to safety.

I have decided "but if not," I will obey.

When Jesus' disciples had been fishing all night without success, Jesus told them to again let down their nets. This did not make any sense. It was not logical or reasonable. The command was not fathomable or responsible. It was probably the last thing they wanted to do. Yet Simon responded, "Master...because you say so, I will..."[9]

Because my master tells me to live this life, I will.

> **"** *Because my master tells me to live this life, I will.*

I still maintain, "For the LORD is good and his love endures forever; his faithfulness continues through all generations."[10]

My losses are substantial and life is completely different now, but it does not mean that my life is over. I still believe the Lord is good and his faithfulness continues.

He remains patient with me and continues to mold and shape me into his masterpiece.[11]

Counting the Cost

By Debbie's friend Dionne

"But it's not fair!" my son whines at me, reciting a list of grievances he holds against his brothers. Injustices he holds against the way we parent. I begin to explain the reason behind my decision, meeting his unreceptive ears. In his age-appropriate immaturity, he is unable to understand my reasoning and good intentions for him.

"It's not fair, but it is producing good character," I say. But even as I explain myself, a nagging question lingers in the back of my mind. "Is this what God is saying to me as well? Am I, in my immaturity, unable to understand his reason for the events in my own life?" Accepting that is relatively easy for myself. My life has had only minor setbacks and struggles, but what about Debbie? How could God possibly have her best intentions at heart as I consider her hardships, her growing disability, her limitations? I find myself saying, "But it's not fair!"

I had a general acquaintance with Debbie for years, with Phil working in the school system and through small town connections. But our paths officially crossed the fall of 2012 when my husband and I and our two young boys moved back to our original Kansas home. With our kids' similar ages, children's activities and playdates quickly grew our friendship. I knew Debbie had been diagnosed with MS, but evidence of that diagnosis was far from my recognition. She did what she wanted, amazed me at how she could juggle kids, an antique/

refinishing business, and the process of adopting Laura. I knew Debbie loved Jesus. She spoke of and demonstrated her faith in her kindness to and caring for others. We developed routines of time together centered around our kids and stay-at-home mom schedules. Her looming disability was far from my mind.

But that changed rapidly throughout the school year of 2017 to 2018. As her youngest two began kindergarten, I welcomed my fourth child into the world. Just as our natural meet-up times waned, so did Debbie's mobility. On the other hand, I felt that our depth of friendship began to grow. No longer was it only based on the natural interactions of caretaking and the woes of early motherhood, but there was a heightened urgency to our discussions and heaviness that could only be processed in the light of Christ.

That year was hard to watch. It was hard to lean in. It was and remains hard to know what it means to be a good friend to Debbie. Watching Debbie become disabled has caused me to question what kind of friend I am. Am I only a friend in the easy times? Am I only a friend for what I gain in the relationship? What does being a good friend as part of the body of Christ look like? I confess, I tend to get caught up in my own life and forget to check in on her. Out of sight, out of mind is my tendency. Thankfully, the Holy Spirit brings Debbie and family to mind often. Reminding me to be a good friend, to pray, to reach out. To just show up. I've never regretted stopping by Debbie's. Maybe it was just for a moment or for a longer chat, but being a good friend requires time, and I'm thankful for the ways I've been shown that through Debbie's disability.

So, I return to the nagging question in my mind, "What good could possibly come out of Debbie's growing disability?" It doesn't take me long to consider the ways in which I've seen God's faithfulness and demonstration of his power through this trial.

First and foremost, I see joy. Demonstration of joy that surpasses the momentary trials. A demonstration of joy that remains even in the heartbreak. It's not the absence of sadness and it is not the ignorance of reality. It is a joy that is untouchable and not based on circumstances. It is the joy only Christ can give. Debbie reminds me of the psalmist David. David often cries out to God, but before he finishes his lament, he remembers the blessing of God. He recalls and meditates on the goodness of God. Debbie has learned the strength in that. There are times I visit Debbie and she is having a hard day. She shares her laments, but she finishes with recalling the goodness of God and a declaration of his praises. This brings me hope and confidence in the Lord. Hope and confidence that I too, through Christ, will be able to handle whatever comes my way with the joy of the Lord as my strength.

Secondly, I've grown to admire confident humility and all it brings. Debbie, once a fiercely independent person, now must humbly ask for help with so many things. When in public, Debbie's disability is not easy to hide. Additional attention given to her wheelchair requires a great deal of humility and confidence on Debbie's part. Listening to Debbie describe her struggle with this tension has grown my heart to release more of my ideals and walk more confidently in who God has made me to be, faults and weaknesses and all.

Finally, another beauty in the ashes has been watching and participating with Debbie as she grows as a prayer warrior. I appreciate her cutting right to the heart of the matter, her intentionality in conversation. Cutting through the fluff right to the rich stuff. I'm encouraged by her describing the hours she devotes to prayer and the riches of time spent with Jesus. Listening to Debbie pray, I too am drawn into sitting at the feet of Jesus and soaking in his presence. There is a richness there that her new pace of life has enhanced. We still pray for her healing. We still pray for regained mobility. But that is not the focus of Debbie's heart and prayers.

Lord, surely in the heartache, there is more. More good stuff than bad. Thank you for reminding me that your light is better than life. That in you, you turn our darkness to light. That even though we live here for but a moment, this life is not our home. Thank you for the opportunity to see this more clearly through Debbie. Thank you for walking with Debbie every step of her journey, and thank you for allowing me to watch.

It is not fair. But you are good.

It is not fair. But you walk us through.

It is not fair. But you are worthy of our praise.

Thank you for Debbie and Phil's proclamation of this truth even in the trial. Thank you for demonstrating your power to sustain through them. The glory is yours alone. Amen.

CHAPTER 10

A Reluctantly Grateful Student

"If I had a choice, I would still choose to
remain blind...for when I die, the first face
I will ever see will be the face of my blessed
Saviour."

–Fanny Crosby

How are you?

We start so many conversations with this loaded question. It
may be simply said in passing or used as a greeting. It may be
asked casually without meaning and without wanting to hear
a genuine answer. Or it may be asked sincerely with the desire
to hear a real, transparent answer.

But do we want the answer to always be "fine" because it may
be uncomfortable if the reply is different? Or do we really
want a truthful response? Every time you and I are asked this
question, we are pressed to consider this dilemma—should
I use an automatic reaction, or should I use an honest, but
potentially awkward, reply? I dread being asked how I am
doing, and I wish it wasn't a part of our culture's everyday
conversation.

The answer is conditional.

How I respond depends on how well I know the person who is asking.

If my relationship with the asker is minimal, I give a vague response. I refuse to lie. Even the misnomer "white lie" is wrong and disobedient to the Lord's desires.

When asked how I am doing, I never know whether I am being asked about my physical self or my emotional well-being. Physically, I'm obviously not doing well. It's hard to want to be honest about my physical situation because the time our conversation has may not lend itself to the weight and seriousness of the situation. Or I may not feel the asker is ready for a transparent answer.

When good friends ask how I am doing, I know they are wanting to know how I am doing emotionally. They know exactly how I'm doing physically. They aren't afraid of my honesty or tears, and I expect them to respond with the same honesty and emotion regarding their own situations.

Appropriate answers to the infamous question are, "I'm good because the Lord is good" and "Better than I deserve." Though these statements are true, my teary eyes may sometimes seem to be a contradiction. Crying belies the indisputable fact that being a part of the Lord's kingdom certainly *is* better than I deserve. I am not a fair-weather fan of the Lord's answers, even if they do not align with my preferences. Again, don't mistake the show of emotion to mean a lack of strength!

> " *Don't mistake the show of emotion to mean a lack of strength!*

As I look back upon my life before The Decline, I wonder if I was not as approachable as I could have been. It may have appeared as if I had it all together as a mom of three young kids, all close in age. Though life was stressful because of the timing of their ages, the weight of mothering rarely showed. Doing life well and efficiently was a primary goal, as was quality time spent with my children. Knowing my own children were my primary ministry opportunity, I was pleased with their polite and respectful behavior. Although I am still proud of my kids' personalities, my routines at that time were very different from what they are now.

Before The Decline, I relished waking up at 5:00 a.m. for my daily run, often silently rehearsing memorized Scripture during the exercise. Once home, I was sure to finish my shower, hair, and makeup before my kids woke up. I enjoyed planning a weekly menu and grocery list.

Accompanying the scheduled planning of meals, I adhered to a timetable of house cleaning and laundry. I almost always folded and put away the clean clothes the same day they were washed. My goal was to do the same with the dishes, and this was met most of the time. I repurposed treasures through fixing and painting for my antique business during my kids' nap times. Their television time was scheduled to happen while I prepared supper. My flower garden stayed weeded and in symmetry, and I meticulously kept my house picked up. On Sundays, we attended an early church service thirty miles away, and each of my children wore appropriate clothing—either a skirt or dress or the boys wore a pair of church pants, non-logo shirts, and dress shoes.

These habits aren't inherently wrong, but my motivation for them was. The ways of achieving these routines were. Although I had my children under control, my transparency was lacking. I was reluctant to be candid; when asked how I was doing, I always smiled and said "good." Though life was very full I was not likely to share my struggles with anyone except the Lord. Authenticity with everyone else was rare.

I had known the Lord my whole life, it seemed, as being a pastor's kid allowed for lots of time spent around the church building. This faith started to become personal in high school, and then even more so toward the end of my college years and into graduate school and married life. Dealing with fertility issues taught me to be disciplined about spending time with the Lord, reading his word and praying, as well as relying on him to be my fortress in difficult times. However strong, this relationship became a bit strained when my children were ages four, two, and one, partly because I felt I didn't have the amount of time needed to spend time quietly in prayer. At that time, I began to show a smiling face no matter what was going on. Reaching out for someone to disciple me was a crucial step to take. As I learned how to listen to the Lord and how to be dedicated about my time spent in prayer, I became too regimented in other areas.

I was still in control and could plan my life. Or so I thought.

Any control I possessed before The Decline regarding my appearance, or the appearance of anything in my responsibility, became a loss. If I previously had been concerned about doing what *I* thought was correct, once The Decline began, I had trouble giving it priority. I learned this lesson from the Lord—to be willing to give up my plans, schemes, and methods. This admonition led to humility, a lesson I haven't enjoyed being taught, but it is necessary for the kingdom. I am no longer able to be such a goal-oriented, scheduled, efficient, and disciplined person.

> **❝** *I was still in control and could plan my life. Or so I thought.*

Having an obvious disability makes me more approachable now in general and at ministry events. Ever since publicly discussing my disability at women's ministry events when using a mobility aid, many more women have reached out to me with questions or comments about faith, trust, and relationship.

This is quite surprising to me, and it is evident that being transparent about difficulties seems real and genuine. Listeners seem to gravitate toward openness because they probably have had something go wrong in their lives as well. Haven't we all?

My disability is obvious, but we *all* have something either hidden or visible that is difficult to handle. I am sorry hardship is inevitable. But connecting with another who has either a similar or different difficulty is beneficial. Hopefully it is comforting to know that someone so obviously affected by the difficulties of life can have peace.

Even when I was a college student, I recognized these feelings of contentment and peace. When I was a young co-ed, my work-study job in the school library put to good use my growing skills of efficiency and organization. A young man who was blind often walked through the building using a cane for guidance, and he was always willing to converse. He amazed Beth, who also worked there, and me by having the ability to tell us apart by the sound of our voices. I don't know if this young man had a relationship with the Lord, but he genuinely seemed to have peace on a consistent basis.

⚘

I want that same routine peace. Just after Jesus admonishes Peter by saying, "you do not have in mind the concerns of God, but merely human concerns,"[6] he challenges his followers by saying if they want to be his disciples, they must "deny themselves, take up their cross and follow me."[7] Self-denial must be the start of lasting peace and keeping in mind the concerns of the Lord. Putting ourselves and our own wills last is necessary in order to be followers of Jesus, and it's difficult for me most of the time. Application of this requirement is hard; fortunately, I get to practice often. The home is the most important place for me to form the habit of selflessness—all spouses get to practice putting others first, and parenting is also a definite test of self-denial. Bypassing the biggest cookie and playing others' favorite music while traveling are just a few examples.

When it comes to being selfless, having a disability provides endless opportunities because it requires humility. It takes denial of my own timing and preferences when I wait for others to push my wheelchair, when I ask for help in a restroom, or when I am left by myself at social events.

⁂

Besides developing humility, one of the bright sides of having a visible disability are the offers of help I receive, and I have learned to accept this support, whether it's wanted or unwanted. There is no room for pride in this area. I do indeed need help with many things, and I'm thankful for others' aid. It is their way of serving, and I don't want to be a thief of their joy. I don't want to hamper an opportunity for them to use talents from the Lord. Gifts the Lord has given should be used.

Help I have received has been both financial and physical. It has come through labor, tangible gifts, meals, and taking my place in the kitchen. More specifically, it has come through leaf-raking, weeding, baking, lifting boxes, carrying furniture, and even painting. It includes installing lighting, vacuuming, deep cleaning, transporting my kids, running errands, and grocery shopping. Assistance has come in the forms of giving me rides, taking me to appointments, and painting my nails. The list is endless; these are beautiful examples of grace, which is defined as the giving of gifts I don't deserve.

Because of the type and amount of help I receive, I have gotten used to many people, without announcement, walking into my home through a perpetually unlocked door. Though this clearly has the potential of feeling intrusive and occasionally can be a loss of privacy, my concern is elsewhere. My privacy is not my top priority. The inclusion of yet another person into my home did not faze me even when I considered home health care before the intravenous steroids were given. I have grown accustomed to accepting help, and when I see it as a necessity, I especially welcome it. I am thankful for the physical help in particular, as this is the primary area in which I need assistance.

Only on one weekend, I did not get the help I needed. In the fall of 2019, I traveled south a few states with my sister and friends to the oldest and largest continually operating flea market in the United States. I rented a motorized scooter because of the stamina needed for the shopping area size, though back at home in most places, I was using a cane with difficulty at that time. Many other people attending the event rented scooters as well—not because of physical need, but because of the huge range of the flea market. As a middle-aged woman without a visible disability using a scooter, I definitely did not appear to need help. This is probably the reason why other shoppers did not make any effort to assist me. In my short time of disability, this is the only location where people have not politely held doors open or given up their place in line. Though I don't expect help, and I hope I do not take assistance for granted, I note and appreciate the relief when it happens.

Help from the Lord is absolutely necessary every minute of the day. Just because my prayers aren't answered in the way I desire, it does not mean the Lord is not coming to my aid. This relief often does not come in ways I recognize, but I know he is always present. He is always hovering over me just as the sun always hovers over us, even on an overcast day when it is not visible. The Lord would cross the ocean for me—he just does not use the path I would take. I must trust the direction he is taking is better than my idea. I must trust his direction makes more sense. After all, his ways are different than mine. His ways are better than mine. In fact, his ways *surpass* mine.

The writer of the hymn "Take My Life and Let It Be," Frances Havergal, calls it a "consecration hymn"—one which shows commitment of all possessions, and even whole person, to the Lord for his purposes. She goes on to express this commitment is what each of us should desire, even at times we see vast differences between the words of the song and our actual feelings. It is at those times we must sing it in hope and faith. "I Am Trusting Thee Lord Jesus" was a hymn also written by Havergal and known to be her favorite when she died at the age of forty-two. The hymn is based on Jeremiah 17:7 (NKJV), "Blessed is the man who trusts in the LORD, and whose hope is the LORD." The biblical definition of hope is a confident expectation of what the Lord has promised. Do I expect what he promises? Can I trust what he says in his word, though sometimes it certainly does not look like it? At this point, I must believe what the Lord says. I must have hope. When 2 Corinthians 1:20 says the Lord's promises are Yes and Amen, I must trustfully, and without doubt, agree.

Jesus says that his yoke is easy.[1] However, the yoke of disability is burdensome, and I will gladly let the Lord take the heaviest half. My half is too hard some of the time. My body resists sitting all day. Staying home is occasionally confining. Not being able to fully control my lower body can cause awkward involuntary jerks. Some days, it is wearisome to put a smile on my face. Comments and stares from others are sometimes too difficult for me to bear. Occasionally, they don't roll off my back quickly enough.

It *must* be better for the Lord's kingdom that I am disabled. Just because I can say this does not mean it is easy to ingest, easy to apply, or easy to live out. In fact, some of the time I think or act as if this is not true. I worry, wish my life was different, and get angry. I get weary of life being so hard, and I get frustrated I can't do even small tasks.

> ❝ *It* must *be better for the Lord's kingdom that I am disabled.*

※※

But beware. Scavenging and snooping around us and our loved ones is our enemy, the devil. He has no truth in him, and he spends his time attacking those on earth. He attempts to rob us of joy and destroys our confidence. Sometimes he is successful, but sometimes not. The Lord has the upper hand, thankfully. Knowing this, early in the years of The Decline, I brazenly said "Bring it on" to the enemy, thinking I could handle anything. Later, as my physical health continued to get worse, I wanted to take it back. I regretted it. I was sorry I had said it. However, now, I am embarrassed that I originally was embarrassed about stating that challenge. When I said "Bring it on," worse things did happen, but I don't need to regret this statement—because the victory belongs to the one who rides across the heavens to help me.[2] The Lord overcomes all. After all, he even has an angel set up a circle of protection around me![3]

Often when hearing a song that has lyrics about healing or about how the Lord is a healer, I don't sing along. I am silent during these parts of songs. I don't disagree the Lord heals, but it hasn't happened in my own life. It is almost as if I feel the room's eyes on me, inquiring how I could possibly sing those words because it obviously isn't true for *me*. I know my imaginings probably aren't true, but it is hard for me to focus at these times. Sometimes kind strangers must think I need to be reminded the Lord heals because they take time to point out his power and miracles. At instances like this, I must focus on the kindness and be thankful for their belief.

I am very familiar with the numerous stories of healing in the Bible. In Acts, healing sometimes occurred because of faith,[4] as is true with the hemorrhaging woman and two blind men in the same chapter of Matthew.[5] Most likely, in part, because of out-of-context reading of these verses, it has been said to either my husband or me that I don't have enough faith to be healed. This extremely offensive belief is hurtful to one who is faithful.

> **"** *It has been said to either my husband or me that I don't have enough faith to be healed. This extremely offensive belief is hurtful to one who is faithful.*

Comments like this only serve to make me feel guilty, shameful, and inadequate—and in the end, angry and offended. I am dedicated to the Lord. No one has the right or responsibility to measure my faith. When confronted with these misdirected thoughts, I often recall a verse from the same book of Matthew, which says, "...For he gives his sunlight to both the evil and the good, and he sends rain on the just and the unjust alike."[6] The Lord gives both good and bad times to everyone, even those who lived in Bible times. Job "...was honest inside and out, a man of his word, who was totally devoted to God and hated evil with a passion."[7] Living in Uz, modern-day southern Israel and Jordan, Job was beset with countless losses—children, property, and health, to name some. Despite emotional and physical pain, Job still said, "...may the name of the LORD be praised."[8]

<hr />

"Give thanks in all circumstances,"[9] we are told. Does this mean I should be thankful for my MS, or does it mean I need only to always be thankful for the lessons I have learned through The Decline? A note in my handwriting next to this verse in my Bible says I should be thankful not *because of* the situation, but *in spite of* it. This makes more sense to me. My thankfulness should not depend upon my circumstances or feelings; when I am obedient to the Lord, it is easier for me to be grateful.

Despite being in a wheelchair all day, which has caused untold grief and taken considerable adjustment, I am still thankful for the benefits. It is not the worst thing that could happen. There are now wheelchair ruts in the carpet, but the flooring can be replaced. Everything seems to take twice as long, so I am forced to develop ways to complete tasks creatively. I sit constantly; nevertheless, it is now easier for my daughter to cuddle in my lap. Though I am not thankful for my multiple sclerosis, I recognize the random benefits. This is assuredly something for which to be thankful.

I do not claim to know what the Lord is doing in this life-changing experience, but one of the purposes must be to teach the crucial lessons I have learned.

Few things now bother me, and I have learned to be flexible and adapt to change quickly and easily.

I also now consider myself laid-back. I do not get offended easily, and unwanted situations do not aggravate me like they did in the past.

I am more patient, and I am likely to not mind waiting. Whether welcomed or not, being disabled forces me to be forgiving and understanding while waiting and not to be concerned by situations that don't go the way planned.

> " *I do not claim to know what the Lord is doing in this life-changing experience, but one of the purposes must be to teach the crucial lessons I have learned.*

Perhaps this is why my family was given a first-time server at a busy restaurant when on vacation. Waiting tables in a famous, and therefore busy, eating establishment can be stressful, and this mix of stressors may result in first-time mistakes, so maybe the operators knew that families having one who is disabled are patient, understanding, and polite. Perhaps this is not true, but one should recognize that those with disabilities, by way of necessity, tend to be uncomplaining and nonjudgmental.

The Lord has also taught me lessons in public recognition and receiving accolades. Because of shyness, I faded into the woodwork in a large high school, but both during college and later, I loved the attention of others and their affirmation after speaking in public. This fondness of being in the spotlight did not end in humility. Using The Decline, the Lord took away avenues of speaking publicly, as I spent energy coping with the changes. Chances to speak in front of others became slim as I slowly disengaged from the public eye because of our time spent at Cottonwood and adjusting to my new normal. However, after re-evaluating priorities throughout this time, opportunities to speak are starting to become available again. Was the Lord waiting for me to be in the right emotional place? Was he waiting for me to give glory to him for all he has done? Am I now better equipped to be his mouthpiece?

"I used to wander off until you disciplined me; but now I closely follow your word. You are good and do only good; teach me your decrees."[10] The Lord is good and does *only good*!? Did the Lord give me the ability to speak publicly for such a time as this? Is my testimony of salvation sweeter now because I have tasted deep sorrow? Would I experience the peace and joy of the Lord if I didn't know hurt and brokenness?

⁂

I experienced brokenness early in an adoption process before we were parents. We had a chance to domestically adopt a newborn before we had children of our own. We spent nearly forty-eight hours in the world of a neonatal intensive care unit (NICU) because Baby C's birth mother had gestational diabetes. He was of average stature, but his organs needed time to fully develop. We experienced Baby C making efforts to suck a miniature bottle, and we loved the skin-to-skin contact. During restless nights in the nearby house utilized for families of hospitalized patients, I turned to my Bible. I was assured by reading verses that helped me assume I would be the mother of Baby C. When the adoption fell through after almost two days, I was surprised, grieved, angry, and confused. But I had been reading the Lord's word literally, not in context. This literal reading led me to think I would get whatever I wanted.

> " *When the adoption fell through after almost two days, I was surprised, grieved, angry, and confused.*

"Whatever you ask in my name, this I will do, that the Father may be glorified in the Son. If you ask me anything in my name, I will do it." John 14:13-14

"If you abide in me, and my words abide in you, ask whatever you wish, and it will be done for you." John 15:7

"Ask, and it will be given to you; seek, and you will find; knock, and it will be opened to you. For everyone who asks receives, and the one who seeks finds, and to the one who knocks it will be opened." Matthew 7:7-8

"And whatever you ask in prayer, you will receive, if you have faith." Matthew 21:22

"You did not choose me, but I chose you and appointed you that you should go and bear fruit and that your fruit should abide, so that whatever you ask the Father in my name, he may give it to you." John 15:6

But we left the NICU without a baby. What we desperately wanted had not been given to us. Our arms were empty. We had lost our baby, and we were defeated.

I had been certain I was finally going to become a mother, so I learned an important lesson that day about how the Lord works. My confusion cleared as I read through the book of Psalms: "for he satisfies the thirsty and fills the hungry with good things"[11] and "The lions may grow weak and hungry, but those who seek the LORD lack no good thing."[12] I wondered whose meaning of good mattered the most. I wondered if my definition of good would prevail, but my definition of "good" was becoming a mother. Becoming Baby C's mother *seemed* like a good thing for me, but it was not ideal for the Lord's kingdom. Though I will never fully know why becoming a mother at that time was not the best fit in the Lord's tapestry, I trust that he always does the right thing at the right time.

Five months later, I was miraculously pregnant with my oldest son.

> **❝** *Though I will never fully know why becoming a mother at that time was not the best fit in the Lord's tapestry, I trust that he always does the right thing at the right time.*

The Lord always does the right thing at the right time. This is apparent in the timing of The Decline. When it began, I was not working out of the home after being a school social worker for eleven years and staying home with my children for nine. The Decline started exactly at the point my youngest children went into kindergarten, which is also an age at which children are more independent. Though I have loved mothering during every phase of childhood, this finally meant no more diapers or tying kids' shoes. No more wiping noses or picking out clothes. We moved on to communication with three teachers and paying attention to class schedules, school happenings, and homework; a torrent of school papers and lunches were launched. I had been warned when I was a mother of babies and toddlers that parenting changed from being physically exhausting to becoming emotionally wearing as they aged, and this unquestionably happened.

Gone were the days of physical fatigue from being a mother— for the first time in ten years, I got to stay still while my kids explored at the park playground. They were now old enough to go from one piece of play equipment to another by themselves, and it did not matter that my mobility prevented me from easily moving around on uneven ground.

Evidence of the Lord's perfect timing abounded. One year before the Decline, The Vintage Soiree, the antique business I co-owned for ten years, was dissolved. My business partner and I closed the business via a mutual decision not based on health reasons, but instead on children's increasing activities. It was difficult to close this chapter, though my colleague and I have since agreed it would have been impossible to keep up with the complicated state of our schedules while maintaining a business with hard work, organization, and fresh ideas. The Lord knew what was coming. He was preparing the way ahead of me.

> **❝** *The Lord knew what was coming. He was preparing the way ahead of me.*

My life has turned almost completely upside down. But no matter what the world says, I am supposed to be a "peculiar"[13] person who tells others of the difference the Lord has made in my life. Becoming disabled is an immense change from how my life used to be. Maybe living life well from a wheelchair does tell others of this difference.

Living life well hopefully proves to others I am defined only by the Lord, not by my wheelchair, walker, or cane. To them, it may seem as if my experience in this world has become disappointing. I am not convinced of this. The Lord doesn't see disappointment. He sees purpose. He sees no regrets.

I want to live a life of no regrets. I want to be in this world, but not of it.[14] I do not pay attention to television, news, or blogs. Though I have one social media account, I miss many big announcements because of my lack of time dedicated to scrolling. Staying current with national and world events has many advantages. But I have other things to do. Other activities may or may not have involved chasing down the family dog in my motorized wheelchair, armed with a leash, dog treats, and my grabber for pushing the garage door button on the wall. (Though quite challenging and comical, our dog was safely returned to the backyard.) I desire spending time with the Lord and in relationship with people.

Living a life of no regrets becomes difficult as I reflect upon the question of perhaps doing life differently if I would have known I wouldn't be able to walk well after 2017. Unquestionably, I would have spent more time exploring, hiking, camping, biking, and kayaking. I would have run with my kids and taken time to teach them to snow ski. I would have even taken the time myself to snow ski with Phil. Maybe I even would have accomplished the long-held dream of skydiving.

Instead, because of my multiple sclerosis, the Lord has caused me to spend ample time alone with him during the school day.

Can I be satisfied with my relationship with the Lord but still hunger for more?

Can I experience grief and joy at the same time?

Can I grieve considerably and still be walking in obedience?

How do I chase after healing while being content with my situation?

How do I pursue a ministry based on being in a wheelchair while still desiring healing?

How do I teach my kids, through significant emotion, that the Lord is good?

Is the Lord's desire for me to be disabled because it draws others to him?

Is the enemy purposely attacking my family as we gather people on Sundays for a house church?

"…Shall we accept good from God, and not trouble?"[15]

Can I say with Job, "Though he slay me, yet will I hope in him…"?[16]

Even more debatable and confusing—is this present suffering a sign of the Lord's love for me?

While I could assume life as a Jesus follower would be easy, I can't ignore portions of the Bible I may wish don't apply to me. Some of these parts could cause dread. But I can't disregard James, the brother of Jesus, when he says, "Consider it pure joy, my brothers and sisters, whenever you face trials of many kinds, because you know that the testing of your faith produces perseverance. Let perseverance finish its work so that you may be mature and complete, not lacking anything."[17]

I don't want to lack anything. I want to be mature and complete.

As hard as it is to suddenly become disabled, God *is* good!

My hope is not shaken.

> " *I don't want to lack anything.*
> *I want to be mature and complete.*

Adjusting to Plan B

By Debbie's mother-in-law Joan

I remember when Debbie first began to have symptoms of MS, which then turned into a diagnosis. It was soon after she graduated from college, which was when she was in Topeka. Phil and she had been dating a few years, and the family was quite sure this lovely girl had a strong bond with him. They learned as much about the illness as they could, and as they decided to put it in God's hands, they knew he would guide and direct them. And, of course, he did.

Long ago, I had a hospice patient with MS, and then we had a pastor whose wife had MS. They didn't have access to the medications at that time that others do now. These medications have been available for the last several years, but Debbie's diagnosis was still a concern because I had seen the results of multiple sclerosis. However, not only did Phil and Debbie share a strong faith in their Savior, he gave them a special love for each other that would carry them through marriage.

I was not surprised the diagnosis didn't affect Debbie for so many years because I knew the Lord can heal, and I also knew the disease could go into remission. I also assumed at that time the medication held off any evidence of MS.

Debbie has always been a giving and thoughtful person, and she always puts the happiness of others first. Through her time spent in a wheelchair, she has taught me to be more tolerant of other people and their situations.

I have known people with disabilities off and on during my life, and I have been amazed at how they can overcome situations. Debbie is the same way. While it would certainly be nice if business places had automatic doors, this is often not true. While others haven't always offered to help, often there are several people who are willing to be of assistance. As someone who uses a walker, learning to go to "plan B" is helpful.

When I think about what Debbie is dealing with, I realize she always has a smile on her face, and she continues to be an inspiration to many. I keep learning from her example. When the Lord closes a window, he then opens another. Whatever we deal with in life, the Lord will guide us.

EPILOGUE
The Story Goes On

As of May 2021, The Decline has stopped. This is possibly due to the intravenous steroids I received at that time. It may be credited to starting a disease-modifying treatment (DMT), the once-a-month injection, at basically the same time. It might be because of an as-yet undiscovered avenue the Lord has provided in order to deliver relief. I will never know, and it is not worth the time spent wondering the cause. After experiencing a new loss every week for four years, at times even more frequently, I feel as if I have a new lease on life. An even newer pair of glasses. I feel as though I can breathe a sigh of relief.

With this sense of reprieve, I'm more carefree in life. I'm more likely to leave the house. I am probably going to attend my kids' school events. I even plan on taking them to a concert. The public seems to be increasingly likely to pay attention to me and listen to my thoughts and opinions. Is this because they're used to seeing me in a wheelchair? Is it because they now know I'm still cognizant? Is it freeing for both them and me to recognize the opportunities for conversation? Or was I subconsciously rebuffing this interaction all along?

Because of my feelings of joy, peace, and contentment, perhaps I am now more openly receptive to others. I have made new friends and recently have discovered connections to ministries and resources. No matter the reason for the end of The Decline, I remain content, and I experience cautious satisfaction. Only the Lord knows his reasoning for The Decline. Though his explanation remains mysterious and I accept that I will probably never understand the reason, I trust the Lord has it all under control.

> **"** *I have a new lease on life.*

Of course, I do not know how long this alleviation will continue. Of course, fear of the future still tempts me. Of course, it bothers me that I am not able to be the wife and mother I had hoped.

This book is written from a strong desire to have a loud voice and to use it for the purpose of giving the Lord thanks, even in demanding times. Though trying times present differently now, they persist. Frequently, I wonder if inflammation is once again attacking the nerves in my brain. Is slight weakening a result of no longer avoiding inflammatory foods? Is it caused by the minimal use of exercise bands and dumbbells? Though only Phil and I notice the faltering, I speculate about repeating the intravenous steroids. This leads to communicating with my neurologist about the next steps and what to expect.

I experience new MS-related sensations frequently. Other unusual symptoms of the disease seemingly come out of nowhere.

Tightening around my lower legs makes it seem as if I always have on tights.

Prickly, scratchy feelings on my hips come and go.

I have light purple feet that are swollen often.

There are times I can't move my left foot off the floor as much as the day before.

Some days my lower body shakes when I stand.

Frequently, I get tired earlier in the day than usual.

Slight blurriness seems to be the norm in my left eye. My eye doctor has told me I may not see perfectly clearly again. Comparable to efforts at finding a radio station amidst static, my vision prescription is tweaked the best it can be.

Though these symptoms are intermittent and vary in severity, they remind me I am not out of the woods. I will probably always have something to which I must quickly adapt. My neighbor might see me on the ground in my driveway and again pick me up. My friend might need to help me to my feet again when trying to walk in her narrow hallway. However, the Lord is sovereign, and I look to him for answers about the next dose of steroids or perhaps a different path he wants me to take. I do not overlook even controversial alternative medicine options anymore.

I have probably made the wrong decisions in the past regarding treatment. I most likely will continue to make incorrect choices as my mind is filled with doubt regarding causes of disease progression. But if I am going to live a life of no regrets, I will instead be thankful for these learning opportunities. These decisions certainly give me practice at listening to the Lord's voice and paying attention to the ways he communicates to me.

> ❝ *If I am going to live a life of no regrets,*
> *I will instead be thankful for these*
> *learning opportunities.*

There is light at the end of the tunnel. After a long period of grief and mourning, joy has returned. Architecture of the Holocaust Museum in Jerusalem depicts this very theme: The infrequent use of light throughout the tunnel-like and seemingly inescapable building is a metaphor depicting truth—beauty does come from ashes. Redemption is enacted by natural light streaming inside from the exit; it is the only light used in the entire museum.

My light at the end of the tunnel shines through precious moments. It may be a wink from a friend as a chair is placed by my wheelchair when I am alone at a social gathering. It may be a stranger, later sharing she has MS, helping me climb a long flight of stairs in an inaccessible building. It may be an imaginable "angel in disguise" taking pictures of our family while sightseeing. It may be a kind smile or thoughtful words.

> " *There is light at the end of the tunnel.*

I must reciprocate. It's tempting to become discouraged and angry because of my physical health, but I have learned these feelings do not improve my situation. It does not help if I glance around with anger when the minimal seats accompanying spots for wheelchairs in a movie theater are occupied by non-disabled patrons when many other places are available. When someone without a disability aid exits a wheelchair-accessible restroom stall while others are empty, it is not beneficial for me to glare, especially if it was a lengthy waiting period. Instead, I will focus on the enjoyable situations I experience. I will smile and laugh.

I smile when I hear the same bird's greeting each morning just before the sun rises. I have grown to love the trills, chirps, and warbles of birds as I pay attention to the Lord's goodness all around me. Discovery and identification of birds intrigues me, and this newfound hobby will serve me well as I age.

In the past few years, I have gotten more compliments, particularly about my appearance, than ever before. Do others not know what else to say? Are they feeling sorry for me because I am in a wheelchair? Because I am very aware my hair is beginning to show more gray and is slowly recovering from post-COVID-19 thinning, I wonder if perhaps these comments are made from feelings of sympathy. In order to put pity to rest, it is my responsibility to show the contentment and peace I genuinely have.

> " *In order to put pity to rest, it is my responsibility to show the contentment and peace I genuinely have.*

Please don't feel sorry for me. Being in a wheelchair doesn't keep me from having enjoyable times.

On a girls' night out recently, several friends alternated helping with my wheelchair. A different friend brought my chair to the van door every time we entered and exited the vehicle, helping me into it and then pushing it. How did they choose? Did they discuss this rotation? The answers are inconsequential; going along was a privilege and a joy.

Weekly distribution of snack items at our local school to show appreciation for all staff members has been part of my schedule recently. I have enjoyed participating in giving thanks to school employees. They deserve it. My involvement shows others I will still be active despite my mobility, and I will have sincere joy at the same time. Though my participation is not always needed, and I have exerted effort to excuse myself because of not wanting to burden others to push my chair during these times, my thoughtful friends have insisted on my participation, denying their own comfort; I treasure their love and persistence.

Not long ago, my husband and I were honored to teach about marriage at a Bible study. This was a wonderful opportunity to merge our speaking styles and continue fine-tuning the art of working together. The chance to portray what the Lord has done in our lives was invigorating.

After this study, an attendee challenged me to be a thoughtful steward of the position I have in life. Disability has been an agent of the Lord's provision and love.

In the recent past, I had the privilege of being a guest on a podcast that encourages others to see beyond what is visible. This enjoyable experience is hopefully not an isolated situation. It was exciting to publicly broadcast the goodness of the Lord.

As I continue to dwell in hope, I will keep moving forward with life.

I will revel in the goodness, kindness, and love the Lord continues to show me.

I will continue to reconcile my desire for healing with contentment.

I will remain unshakable.

I will still stand.

Reviews are very helpful for independent authors.

Please take a few moments to write a review of this book on a book-selling website.

Thank you!

QUESTIONS FOR
Contemplation and Discussion

INTRODUCTION

1. The title of this section is "A Changed Perspective." Debbie begins to tell how her life has been upended. What is your "changed perspective" story? Do you have any memories of times when your life was altered drastically?

2. Debbie describes how a worship melody came to her mind when lying on the bathroom floor after a fall. Do you have similar reactions to difficult circumstances? What worship songs resonate with you during hard times?

3. The introduction ends on a raw and even combative note while Debbie begins to ask God hard questions about her circumstances. She even questions his goodness! Is that okay?

4. Take a look at Psalm 13. King David, a man after God's own heart (1 Samuel 13:14), is not afraid to shout his dismay toward the heavens. Have you ever expressed doubt or anger honestly in prayer?

CHAPTER 1

1. Debbie's diagnosis of multiple sclerosis was not a complete surprise because of her genetic predisposition—her grandmother also had the disease. Why is it important to know as much about your family medical history as possible? Do you need to do some research in this area?

2. It's hard not to succumb to fear when given a life-altering medical diagnosis. Have you ever been given difficult health news by a doctor? What was the circumstance and how did you react?

3. Debbie remembers asking the Lord to develop patience in her when she was younger, and then she recounts painful instances where he allowed her to experience that character trait. Have you ever asked for patience and had it come about in a way you would not have expected?

4. Debbie begins: "This is a story of waiting. But it's also a story of undying hope." What are some things you are waiting and hoping for today? How do you push past the disappointment in the long wait?

5. Every chronic disease has non-profit foundations that raise money for research and advocacy. Are you involved in any fundraising or volunteer efforts with organizations such as this?

6. Debbie's dad speaks of "godly hindsight" when expressing gratefulness that Debbie's disease did not affect her early life. What is a circumstance you can look

back on with "godly hindsight" and see how the Lord blessed your situation?

CHAPTER 2

1. Debbie currently keeps a journal of her medical history, and she referred often to it while writing *Still Standing*. It reminds her of her many trials and also many blessings. Do you have a written record of the difficulties and redemption the Lord has allowed in your life? Why might that record be a treasure to your children and grandchildren?

2. Debbie fought the increasing use of mobility aids for as long as she could. How difficult do you think it was for her family to watch this stubborn desire to keep things as "normal" as possible? Do you know anyone who is in denial about the level of medical assistance they need? How do you broach such an uncomfortable conversation?

3. As a long-distance runner, hiker, and overall outdoor-loving young mom, Debbie's grief over these lost activities is intense. Have you ever had to give up doing something you loved because of a medical condition? Where have your emotions landed with that process? Are you still angry, sad, or have you come to peace with it?

4. The loss of income opportunities is a real concern for anyone with a disability. How adaptable is your career when it comes to loss of such things as mobility or

sight? Do you work with anyone who has a disability? How does this affect their work and yours?

5. Debbie recounts occasional times during The Decline when she needed assistance and none was given. The problem was not with close friends or strangers, but with casual acquaintances. How would you react if a young mom you did not know well showed up at church in a wheelchair or at your child's ballgame using a walker? Be honest.

6. Debbie talks about developing a "realistic fear" of the future when first starting to deal with The Decline. Is fear a sin? Back up your answer with Scripture. How do you deal with fear of things to come?

CHAPTER 3

1. Almost 30 percent of those receiving government disability income in the U.S. have musculoskeletal issues. Do you know anyone like this? How has it affected their life and that of their family? How can you reach out and be an encouragement?

2. Author Elisabeth Kubler-Ross coined the "five stages of grief" in 1969. These include denial, anger, bargaining, depression, and acceptance, which can come in any order. Debbie's younger brother said he wrestled for a time with denial of her disease but has currently landed on anger. Have you ever experienced any of these grief stages? What was that like?

3. Debbie is blessed with a twin sister who is also her best friend. Do you have a sister or brother—biological or

spiritual—that you can call when things are tough? Can you be that "sibling" to someone in need?

4. While reading *Still Standing*, have you become more aware of accessibility details? What about obstacles for the disabled in your community? What can you do to ensure that those with handicaps can enjoy life outside their homes just as much as you do?

5. Debbie has had to completely reinvent how she lives at home. It has affected everything from where the master bedroom is, to how she gets in the car, and then to how she does her hair and makeup every morning. How would your home have to be altered if you were to suddenly lose full use of your legs and/or arms?

6. While traveling in the Holy Land, Debbie was excluded from several holy sites due to lack of accessibility. How would you feel if you traveled all the way to the Lord's home turf, the trip of a lifetime, and had to sit alone while the rest of your family climbed down steps to Lazarus' tomb? How would you feel if you were prayed for on the very spots where Jesus healed others, but you did not experience healing?

CHAPTER 4

1. What is "normal"?

2. Debbie says the Lord is "not typical, usual, or expected. He is *not* normal." How is he not normal? Why do we strive so hard to be "normal" when he not?

3. Read 2 Corinthians 1:3-4. Debbie talks about crying with friends who are in similar difficult circumstances. Why is it a source of comfort to know someone who has been through what you are going through?

4. Sometimes it is hard to know how to start a conversation with someone who is in a completely different place in life than we are—the disabled, the homeless, the freshly grieving. Debbie says she appreciates when others ask her about her day, her family, or her activities, "just like anyone else." Come up with a list of a half-dozen questions you can use the next time you have the opportunity to bless someone with casual conversation.

5. Debbie states emphatically that she does not believe her disease is punishment from the Lord. In fact, she is horrified anyone would think he operates that way. Have you ever believed you were being punished by God? Do you still believe that? Do a word study on "discipline" versus "punishment" in the Scriptures and ask the Lord to reveal any misunderstandings or lies you have believed about his character.

6. Support groups are available for those who find themselves in any number of hard places in life. Debbie has not yet taken advantage of any MS support groups, although she says she "knows for certain it would be therapeutic." Have you ever benefitted from a support group? What encouragement would you give someone to become involved in one?

PHOTO GALLERY

1. The photos of Grandmother Luella are so poignant, as we know the painful and truncated life that awaits her. What is something you would tell her if you could go back in time?

2. Debbie's parents have a rock-solid faith in the Lord that has helped the whole family during these days of trials with her disease. Ask the Lord to strengthen your faith, so you might enjoy him more today, and also that you might be better prepared for anything the future throws at you.

3. When you look at these pictures of Debbie with friends and family before her symptoms manifested themselves, how does it make you feel?

4. Debbie has obviously determined not to let MS keep her a prisoner at home. Have you ever had difficult circumstances that would have been easier to deal with if you just sat and did nothing? How did you overcome that tendency? How could you encourage someone else to get out and have fun?

CHAPTER 5

1. What is the most painful loss you have ever experienced? How has it impacted your life both negatively and also positively?

2. The phrase "God won't give you more than you can handle" is often misquoted as Scripture. What does

1 Corinthians 10:13 actually say? What other "sound advice" is often mistakenly attributed to the Bible?

3. The Bible tells us that God keeps tabs on every tear that falls. Christ himself is recorded as weeping more than once in the Gospels. Why do you think the Lord allows painful circumstances on earth today when he will eventually wipe away all tears (Revelation 21:4)?

4. Phil and Debbie's disappointments reach beyond her MS to past fertility and adoption struggles. She notes that these troubles resulted in spiritual growth that is bolstering their situation today. Have you had trials which, in hindsight, clearly prepared you for things to come?

5. Debbie admonishes us to avoid inserting our opinions in situations where we have no experience. Even the use of Scripture can be irritating or even painful to someone in a difficult place. How can you apply her advice and learn to "listen, stay quiet, and pray" the next time you are with a grieving person?

6. Lynette states that she's thankful to be involved in Debbie's story "that God is weaving together for good." So far, what good have you seen come out of Debbie's MS narrative? Meditate on Romans 8:28 and ask the Lord to help you love him more.

CHAPTER 6

1. Debbie tells us the divorce rate among those with disabilities is disproportionately high. How can you act to counter that statistic by encouraging and supporting

someone you know who has a family member with a handicap?

2. If you knew that today would be the last day you could walk unassisted, what would you do differently?

3. As The Decline, filled with new struggles daily, hit Phil and Debbie like a tidal wave, she says they neglected to talk to their young sons and daughter in enough detail about what was going on. How would you approach a discussion with children about an unpredictable, chronic disease with no known cure? Is there something going on in your home today that you should be talking to your kids about, but you just don't know where to start?

4. Debbie says she prays her children "experience amnesia" regarding times she has made parenting mistakes. What would you say to reassure Debbie about her parenting if you could sit down and have coffee with her?

5. Read and meditate on Psalm 13 again. How does King David wrap up his cry to heaven?

6. Phil recounts a childhood memory of a Christian man who abandoned his wife after her MS diagnosis. This had a huge impact on his young mind and brought niggling doubts regarding his ability to commit to marrying Debbie. What would you have told young Phil about that situation in order to comfort and encourage him?

CHAPTER 7

1. Is there any difference between happiness and joy?

2. Read Genesis 22:1-18. Have you ever noticed how this story is a literary type, or foreshadowing, of God's sacrifice of his only son? How has Jehovah Jireh (v. 14) made himself known to you? How can you spread the word that the LORD provides?

3. Thankfully, the steroid infusion halted the quickly progressing symptoms of Debbie's MS, and she even regained some function. She remains grateful and excited about this result, even if she is still not walking. How do difficult circumstances in your life cause you to look on the "bright side" of things?

4. Debbie says a favorite verse of hers is Psalm 139:5a: "You hem me in behind and before." Do you have a favorite verse? Have you committed it to memory? Do so today.

5. In this chapter, Debbie begins to unpack the book title, *Still Standing*. How do you feel about the title? How does it tie together everything you have read so far?

6. Carisa says the hardest thing about being Debbie's friend during this time is "a feeling of helplessness." Have you ever felt helpless watching someone in a painful situation? Are we truly helpless when we have an audience with the Creator of the Universe through our Lord Jesus Christ? Pray today for Debbie, her family, and anyone you know who is experiencing trials.

CHAPTER 8

1. Theophan the Recluse was a 17th century Russian Orthodox bishop and author who was canonized in 1988. How does his quote at the beginning of the

chapter resonate with you? Have you had instances when you know God delivered you from trouble through his "unmistakable mercy?"

2. Debbie references the infamous year of 2020. What memories do you have of pandemic life—both good and bad?

3. Just when it seemed things could not get worse, the Oelke family was hit with yet another setback when it was discovered their house needed mold remediation. Their family of five had nowhere to go until the Lord miraculously provided a beautiful country getaway through a good friend. Have you ever had the opportunity to share a blessing like this with someone in need? Did you take the opportunity, or let it slip through your fingers?

4. During this time, Debbie had a stem cell replacement with disappointing results. How hard is it for you to balance anticipation of a prayer answered as you want it to be versus the possibility of a "no" from the Lord?

5. One benefit of the Cottonwood months was Debbie's deliverance from a long-held fear of living in the country. What is a fear you currently struggle with? Do a word study of "fear" in Scripture, beginning with 1 John 4:18, asking the Holy Spirit to teach you what he has for you in these verses.

6. Alaina's essay talks about judging—not condemning, but simply forming an opinion after careful consideration. How do we balance our thoughts about others without

slipping into the type of judging Christ condemns in Scripture? Meditate on Matthew 7:1-3 and talk to the Lord about any feelings of condemnation you hold toward another person.

CHAPTER 9

1. Debbie frames her desperation to be healed "sooner rather than later" through Psalm 90:4 and 2 Peter 3:8. Do those verses revive your desire to ask for things you thought were impossible?

2. If you are currently able-bodied, how has Debbie's story encouraged you to find the energy and determination to use your physical strengths to further the Lord's kingdom? Do you have any areas of disability, or lack of resources, which are discouraging?

3. Do you think those in sincere service to the Lord experience more trials and attacks of the enemy than Christians who are disengaged? Back up your opinions with Scripture references (taken in context!).

4. How can you reframe a negative situation you are in with the "Would You Rather" game Debbie talks about in this chapter?

5. Early followers of Christ were understandably confused when fellow believers experienced illness and death. Imagine for a moment what it would have been like to be in community with those who witnessed Christ's healings and believed he would return very "soon" (there's that word again).

6. Dionne says she is drawn to the feet of Jesus when Debbie prays. Do you have a friend who draws you to the Lord with the depth and sincerity of her prayers?

CHAPTER 10

1. How do you respond when someone asks, "How are you?"

2. Debbie recounts the pride she used to take in her well-organized life, and her tendency not to be honest with others about her struggles raising three young children. How can you be more authentic with friends, acquaintances, and even family this week?

3. "I was still in control and could plan my life. Or so I thought." How do these words resonate with you? What circumstances have reminded you that you are not in control of anything?

4. Jesus said that anyone who wishes to be his disciple must "deny themselves, take up their cross and follow me." Does this clear message fly in the face of our current culture of self-discovery and self-fulfillment? Or can true self-discovery come only through following the Lord?

5. Hymn writer Frances Havergal called "Take My Life and Let It Be" a "consecration hymn," meaning it shows commitment of all we are to the Lord's purposes. Modern worship artist Chris Tomlin has even produced a beautiful adaptation of the hymn. Listen to one or both versions of the song and spend time with the Lord worshipping in spirit and truth (John 4:23-24).

6. Debbie talks about others hurling hurtful accusations at her regarding a lack of faith because of the lack of physical healing. These indictments are often the result of taking Scripture out of context. How important is it for you to take into consideration the whole body of God's word when applying Scripture to your life?

EPILOGUE

1. One thing Debbie has noticed as she spends time in a wheelchair is that others tend to believe she is not cognizant. She admits having the same reaction to others before she lost her mobility. Do you assume someone in a wheelchair is not able to communicate well? How can you go out of your comfort zone the next time you are in a social situation with a wheelchair-bound person?

2. What does the phrase "cautious satisfaction" mean to you? Have you ever, or are you currently, in a place where that makes sense?

3. Debbie describes the symbolism of the Holocaust Museum in Jerusalem as a "light at the end of the tunnel." If you are in dark circumstances right now, what light are you looking toward?

4. Throughout *Still Standing*, Debbie describes how she has experienced a lack of consideration from able-bodied people who use handicapped restrooms or seating. How has this exposure changed your thinking about using space reserved for the disabled?

5. "Please don't feel sorry for me," Debbie urges. How can we move past pity to empathy when it comes to friendships with others in tough circumstances?

6. Reflect on all you have learned after reading Debbie's story and thank the Lord for opening your heart and mind to new ideas. Continue to pray for the Oelke family as they stand strong in the one who created us all.

Acknowledgments

Primary gratitude is due the Lord. He planted the idea of this book in my head, and it has only grown since then. Many times, I have been overwhelmed and felt out of my league, but his loving guidance has always kept me moving forward. Throughout my life, I have occasionally felt like a fish out of water, and writing/publishing a book is no different, but Jesus as my constant companion makes it all bearable and possible.

Love and appreciation without end go to my partner in life, Phil. This journey has been harder than we ever would have suspected, and the difficulty continues to grow. Though the end is not in sight, I know we can continue to travel this path because we are right next to each other, and the Lord is all around us: above, below, in front, behind, to the right, and to the left. He hems us in.

My children are full of forgiveness and mercy—more so than me. Few kids grow up with a mom in a wheelchair; you three excel at this!

Thanks to my parents and siblings. Your interest in and support of this project has been delightful. You've listened to the details of the ongoing process with attentiveness.

As have my friends. Whether or not you have enjoyed hearing about the minutiae of writing, you have courteously paid attention.

To those who have contributed their thoughts–I am especially thankful for you asking the Lord to lead you on this literary venture: Phil, Dad, Mom, Beth, Sarah, Lynette, Alaina, Dionne, Joan, and Carisa.

Thoughts and experiences that were triggered by my questions indeed helped to guide this book. To Tim, Matt, Ashley, Jean, and Karen, I appreciate all of your input.

Without the details of words, images, and design, this book may have remained standard. Thanks for using your God-given gifts: Jessi, Courtney, Jet, Janet, Malinda, Ken, Jennifer, and Emma.

For this project to succeed without the expertise and friendship of my editor, Traci Matt, is laughable.

Sources

Chapter 1

1. Exodus 14:21-22
2. Romans 8:11

Chapter 2

1. 2 Corinthians 12:9
2. Just, Malinda. "Stories: Multiple Sclerosis." Posted March 29, 2019. Malinda D. Just: Encouragement for Foundational Living. www.malindajust.com. (Accessed October 29, 2021.)
3. Ibid.
4. John 5:1-15
5. Luke 8:43-48
6. Psalm 119:68
7. 2 Corinthians 6:4, 10
8. Matthew 11:7

Chapter 3

1. John 2:13-17
2. Matthew 6:12

Chapter 4

1. Matthew 7:14

Sarah

1. John 16:33 ESV
2. Matthew 28:20 ESV

Chapter 5

1. Matthew 14:25
2. Psalm 56:8 NLT
3. Luke 19:41
4. John 11:35
5. Isaiah 66:9 NCV
6. Philippians 3:7 NLT
7. Psalm 119:50 MSG
8. Leviticus 26:13 NLT
9. Psalm 34:15
10. Matthew 5:3-5 MSG

Lynette

1. Matthew 17:20
2. John 9:3

Chapter 6

1. Psalm 13:2 NLT
2. Psalm 13:5 NLT

Phil

1. 1 John 4:19
2. Revelation 21:9
3. Psalm 139:13

4. Ephesians 5:25
5. Matthew 16:24

Chapter 7

1. James 1:2
2. 1 Corinthians 10:13b
3. Matthew 7:11
4. Joel 2:25
5. Psalm 90:15 NLT
6. Psalm 94:18
7. Psalm 94:19

Carisa

1. Psalm 27:13-14

Chapter 8

1. 1 John 4:18
2. Psalm 20:7
3. Isaiah 55:12
4. Luke 19:40
5. Psalm 19:1-3

Chapter 9

1. 2 Peter 3:8
2. Psalm 139:17-18 NLT
3. Judges 6:14
4. Jeremiah 29:7
5. Jeremiah 29:4-7

6. 1 Thessalonians 4:13-14
7. Hebrews 6:19a
8. Daniel 3:17-18
9. Luke 5:5
10. Psalm 100:5
11. Ephesians 2:10 NLT

Chapter 10

1. Matthew 11:30
2. Deuteronomy 33:26
3. Psalm 34:7 MSG
4. Acts 3:16
5. Matthew 9:22, 29
6. Matthew 5:45 NLT
7. Job 1:1 MSG
8. Job 1:21
9. 1 Thessalonians 5:18
10. Psalm 119:67-68 NLT
11. Psalm 107:9
12. Psalm 34:10
13. Deuteronomy 14:2 KJV
14. John 17:11, 16
15. Job 2:10
16. Job 13:15
17. James 1:2-4